OCEAN FREIGHTER FINALE

by

Nigel Jones

The traditional amidships layout freighter ***Egton*** (9958gt) was built by Bartram & Sons Ltd, Sunderland, and completed in 1962 for Rowland & Marwood's Steamship Co Ltd (managed by Headlam and Son), Whitby. At the time of her delivery freight rates were low and no profitable work could be found; thus she was put straight into lay up at Sunderland, which was to last a full year. This was an inauspicious start to her career and a foretaste of a much lengthier period of inactivity to come. In the autumn of 1963 ***Egton*** commenced her belated maiden voyage in ballast to load grain at Comeau Bay, Canada. On 24 January 1967 she sustained serious bottom damage due to grounding at Ness Point, near Whitby, her port of registry. Several hours later she was refloated and dry-docked at Wallsend for examination. Due to complications with the repair work, she did not return to service until July 1967. From September 1972 she was the sole vessel owned by the Whitby firm. Dearth of work forced ***Egton*** into lay up again, this time at Hartlepool, where she arrived in April 1977. She was carefully maintained, which explains her splendid appearance when photographed five years later, on 17 April 1982. Almost four years of idleness passed. With no prospect of work materialising, the ***Egton*** was sold for breaking up; she was towed out of Hartlepool Docks on 6 January 1986 destined for Naantali, Finland. Significantly, ***Egton*** was the last British-owned and registered ship of her type.

INTRODUCTION

British tramp ships, such as Reardon Smith Line's ***Vancouver City*** (7261gt/42), berthed in Cardiff Docks during the early sixties are the backcloth to my earliest shipping memories. The whole shipping scene has radically altered from those times. In particular, the transportation of break-bulk goods by sea has been transformed by the container revolution, resulting in conventional vessels replaced by specialised cellular container ships. Cardiff Docks, like many similar-sized UK ports, has not adapted well to these changes; many years have passed since a fine general cargo ship or reefer, built in the 1950s or 1960s, last visited. Moreover, during this period there have been momentous changes throughout the world. Among the most influential events was the collapse of Communist regimes in Eastern Europe during the 1980s, which resulted in the end of the Eastern Bloc in 1989 and dissolution of the Soviet Union at the end of 1991.

The end of the Soviet Union coincided with the life-expiry of many of its ships built in the 1960s as part of new economic and political realities that necessitated a dramatic expansion of its merchant fleet. This expansion programme included many traditional vessels built by domestic shipbuilders, several of its satellite states (notably East Germany, Poland, and Romania) as well as Yugoslav shipyards. In the 1960s also, the Soviet Union's merchant fleet had been divided into regional groups and companies. Following the Soviet Union's collapse into independent nations the companies, together with the beneficial ownership of the ships, were transferred to these new countries. The transfers were determined by geographical means for example the Black Sea Shipping Company of Odessa was taken over by the Ukraine. However, in the early 1990s generally the new independent nations and the former Soviet satellite states were in a severely poor economic situation and in no position to commence replacing their elderly vessels. Gradually the economies of several of these nations recovered as private enterprise flourished. Privatisation of state-owned merchant fleets progressed, heralding the end for many of the old ships. For enthusiasts of traditional general cargo ships, the 1990s thus proved to be something of an Indian summer: the last chance to see many different types of former Eastern Bloc conventional vessels in service before replacement by new tonnage.

In 1993 I enjoyed a three-day excursion from Limassol to Egypt, which included a day-trip by coach from Port Said to view the famous pyramids of Giza. During the return leg of the coach journey I caught a glimpse in the distance of a line of ships, which seemed to be marooned in the desert but I quickly realised was a northbound convoy of vessels transiting the Suez Canal. This spawned an idea of making an expedition to the Canal, primarily in the hope of seeing plenty of conventional shipping. Further investigation, and help from my good friend Malcolm Cranfield, suggested that vessels could be photographed at standard-lens range, a very appealing prospect. Thus, just before sunrise one morning in mid-June 1994, I found myself standing on the promenade at Port Tewfik, near Suez, wondering what ships would pass by during the course of the day. This venture certainly lived up to expectations and the daily convoys usually included at least a couple of antiquated ships of the former Eastern Bloc, which often tended to appear run-down or rusty. Convinced the era for these superb vessels was rapidly drawing to a close, I made a few more pilgrimages to the Canal in 1995 and 1996 to photograph as many as possible before it was too late.

On one of the very many days of inclement weather during the British summer of 2008, I spent a few happy hours perusing my profusely illustrated reference manuals about Eastern Bloc ships by Ambrose Greenway. I wondered what had happened to the various types of general cargo ships and numerous listed vessels built in the sixties or seventies. I was eager to find out as I had seen quite a few of the ships mentioned on the Suez Canal or at other ports of the world. I therefore decided that these listings would need to be researched; a major project to undertake which developed into an idea to compile this book. Thus, I have determined the fate of many of the general cargo ship types during the two decades since the collapse of the Communist regimes in Eastern Europe. I have expanded the basic concept by coverage of examples of the principal *Liberty Ship Replacement* types and some of the relatively few miscellaneous classic general cargo vessels. Essentially these three categories form the traditional ocean cargo ships' finale. This book is not a definitive account of the subject.

In compiling this book, for expediency purposes, I have used the word freighter in terms of meaning general cargo ship, including multi-purpose ship (Combo) vessel i.e. designed with capacity for both break-bulk cargo and containers. The first section of the book is devoted to the miscellaneous classic ships, the second section deals with ships formerly controlled by Communist regimes in Eastern Europe and the final section dedicated to the *Liberty Ship Replacements* types. As far as possible I have included at least the gross tonnage figure and year of build for each ship mentioned for the benefit of readers who may wish to make more detailed research; the ships' histories are corrected to March 2009. For various reasons the tonnage figure of ships can vary according to the source used and also because ships are subject to remeasurement. Occasionally the rendering of a ship's name is debatable when presentation on the ship differs to the way it is printed in shipping registers.

The majority of vessels I have featured were broken up at Alang in the State of Gujarat, India which in recent times has been made world famous by organisations such as Greenpeace about issues relating to environmental pollution, workforce health and safety etc. Despite such adverse publicity, ships continue to be beached at the demolition plots strung out along miles of shoreline. Sachana is a remote site about five miles from Jamnagar town, also in the State of Gujarat, which has very limited ship breaking capacity.

The pictures selected were taken at various locations world-wide but for reasons mentioned above, the Suez Canal is prominently featured; hence for the purpose of convenience only other locations are mentioned.

Nigel Jones Dinas Powys July 2009

Published by Bernard McCall, 400 Nore Road, Portishead, Bristol, BS20 8EZ, England. Website : www.coastalshipping.co.uk
Telephone/fax : 01275 846178. E-mail : bernard@coastalshipping.co.uk
All distribution enquiries should be addressed to the publisher.

Printed by Amadeus Press, Ezra House, West 26 Business Park, Cleckheaton, West Yorkshire, BD19 4TQ
Telephone : 01274 863210; fax : 01274 863211; e-mail : info@amadeuspress.co.uk; website : www.amadeuspress.co.uk

ISBN : 978-1-902953-44-1

ACKNOWLEDGEMENTS

It would have been impossible for me to create this book without the kind support and co-ooperation of many friends and individuals. I am exceedingly grateful to both David Hazell and Simon Smith for their very valuable and most considerable assistance in the research process. In particular they have helped identify the relatively few ships which are either still in existence or continued existence is in doubt. They have also helped in establishing the ultimate fate of many other vessels.

It is my pleasant task to thank especially Bob Allen, Paul Boot, Malcolm Cranfield, Trevor Jones, Bernard McCall, Peter Melliar, Bill Schell, Graham Thursby, John Wiltshire as well as Captains Stephen Hurlstone, Costas G Kangelaris and Danny Lynch for all their advice, assistance or tips during the past few decades on many aspects of shipping and photography which, however small, in some way has contributed to the making of this book.

The photographs were caught in my own camera unless otherwise stated. I am very grateful for additional material supplied by Paul Boot, Trevor Jones and Simon Smith whose work has been individually credited. Also I much appreciate the generosity of friends who have donated pictures to my own collection.

Again thanks are due to Paul Boot, Malcolm Cranfield, David Hazell and Simon Smith for their detailed checking of the initial draft, suggested corrections and improvements and also my thanks to Gil Mayes for his careful checking of initial drafts of this book.

I am indebted to individuals such as Andy, Iain, Josh and many other acquaintances that I have made locally, on my travels, and through correspondence who, often unwittingly, have given or provided assistance which has had a bearing on the compilation of this book.

I must record that I much appreciate Bernard McCall for taking on this project and for guiding it through to the high quality product which is a hallmark of all his publications.

Many thanks to Amadeus Press for their fine efforts in achieving such a high standard in the printing and presentation of the finished book.

SOURCES USED

British Tramps	I G Stewart
Comecon Merchant Ships	Ambrose Greenway
Deutsche Dampfschiffffahrts-Gesellschaft "Hansa"	World Ship Society
Deutsche Serienfrachter	Gert Uwe Detlefsen
Elder Dempster Fleet History 1952-1985	J Cowden & J Duffy
Liberty Ships in Peacetime	I G Stewart
P&O A Fleet History	World Ship Society
SD14 The Full Story	John Lingwood (Ships in Focus Publications)
Soviet Merchant Ships	Ambrose Greenway
also the following periodicals and websites:	
Lloyd's Register of Shipping	
Lloyd's Shipping Index	
Marine News	World Ship Society
Miramar Ship Index	Rodger Haworth
News Facts & Info	David Hazell
Ships Monthly	Articles by Dr Allan Ryszka-Onions
Ships in Focus Record	Ships in Focus Publications
Sea Breezes	

FLAG ABBREVIATIONS

ATG	Antigua & Barbuda
BHS	Bahamas
BLZ	Belize
BOL	Bolivia
BRB	Barbados
CHN	People's Replublic of China
COM	Comoros
CYP	Cyprus
GBR	United Kingdom
GEO	Georgia
HND	Honduras
IND	India
IRN	Iran
KHM	Cambodia
KNA	St Kitts & Nevis
KOR	South Korea
LBR	Liberia
MLT	Malta
PAN	Panama
POL	Poland
PRK	North Korea
RUS	Russia
SGP	Singapore
SLE	Sierra Leone
SYR	Syria
THA	Thailand
TON	Tonga
TUR	Turkey
UKR	Ukraine
USA	United State of America
VCT	St Vincent & Grenadines
VNM	Vietnam
VUT	Vanuatu

Front cover : During the last few decades of the twentieth century many ocean freighters were prematurely made redundant, replaced by ever more efficient container vessels or bulk carriers, and dispatched to breakers' yards in India, Bangladesh or China. Sometimes there were exceptions when an owner, either optimistic about future prospects or perhaps out of sentiment, instead opted to lay up a ship. A case in point is the Bahamas-registered, British owned, freighter ***Tamamima*** which in July 1998 was laid up in a picturesque setting on Tolverne Reach near Truro, Cornwall, for an exceptionally long period of more than seven years. The ship's skeleton crew did at least undertake basic maintenance sufficient to keep her appearance spruce. She is seen nearly eight months into the lay up on 27 February 1999. Further details of the history of the ***Tamamima*** and subsequent fate are given on the following page.

Back cover : The Panamanian-registered ***Daisy I*** (2723gt/68), formerly ***Tsiglomen***, is seen at Cliff Quay in the port of Ipswich during October 1998. She was one of numerous similar vessels built in Finland during the 1960s and 1970s for the Soviet Union and was designed specially for the timber trades; further details are provided on pages 65 to 67. In 1999 ***Daisy I*** was sold to Georgian-flag interests and renamed ***Simba***; the new owners traded her between ports of the Black and Mediterranean seas. During heavy weather on 12 November 1999 she grounded on sand at Port La Nouvelle in south-west France and was fortunate not to have been wrecked during a protracted stranding. It was perhaps not entirely unexpected that afterwards she was sold to Turkish shipbreakers and arrived at Aliaga on 26 October 2000.

[Author's collection]

During the 1970s a class of twelve freighters fitted with eighteen derricks was built at Sunderland for the well-known British company Bank Line, formed in 1905. The penultimate member of the class, ***Crestbank*** (12238gt) registered at London, was completed in April 1978. She was sold to Tamahine Shipping Ltd in 1986 and temporarily renamed ***Tamathai***. This name was subsequently also carried by the former ***Tenchbank*** (see page 6). In July 1987 she was acquired by Dimitris Manios (Transman Shipping Enterprises) who renamed her ***Northman***. Curiously, less than a year later she reverted to Tamahine Shipping Ltd and was renamed ***Tamamima***, transferring to the Hong Kong and Bahamas registers in the early and middle 1990s respectively. She traded worldwide for Tamahine Shipping until laid up in 1998. The sale of ***Tamamima*** in autumn 2005 was well covered by both the local press and a number of enthusiasts' magazines; there were also reports that she would be scrapped at Gadani Beach. She was renamed ***Berga*** (VCT), pictured on 11 December 2005, and eventually left Tolverne Reach on 19 January 2006. Yet, prior to using the Suez Canal on 8 April 2006, she had had a further change of name to ***Novanoor*** (SLE) following acquisition by United Arab Emirates-based owners for further trading. She was still in service in March 2009 but not long before had changed flag to St. Kitts & Nevis.

In 1977 Bank Line Ltd placed orders with Sunderland Shipbuilders Ltd for six sister ships, known as the *Fish* class, which were each of 12214gt and completed in 1979. In 1983 the ***Ruddbank*** became the first member of the *Fish* class to leave Bank Line's fleet when sold to the Vestey group. During the next eight years she had spells employed on their services in the guises of ***Romney***, then ***Lairg*** and finally ***Napier Star***. In 1991 she became the fourth former Bank Line ship to join the Hong Kong-managed, British-owned, Tamahine Shipping fleet and was renamed ***Tamapatcharee*** (the ***Kowloon Countess*** (10322gt/67), formerly ***Maplebank***, was briefly owned in 1985; also see page 6). She is seen on 26 June 1995 but later that year was sold to South Asia Shipping Ltd, (managed by John McRick & Co Ltd) and renamed ***Lady Rebecca***. In 1998 she was acquired by ITF World Expo Ltd, and became the British-flag ***Global Mariner*** for an unusual role of exhibition ship in the International Transport Workers' Federation's (ITF) flight against flags of convenience shipping and exploitation of seafarers. After completing ITF's round-the-world mission in early 2000 she reverted to commercial service and was also used as a cadet training vessel. Unfortunately, on 2 August 2000 while leaving Matanzas, Venezuela she was in collision with the container ship ***Atlantic Crusader*** (CYP, 7366gt/92). The ***Global Mariner*** quickly sank after her holds flooded. The wreck was moved to a beach in 2001 and sold to a local scrap dealer. She was the last traditional ocean freighter under the Red Duster.

The raised deck aft, deep transom stern, oval section masts and Velle type crane derricks all contributed to the unique appearance of the *Fish* class. The ***Tenchbank*** was not only the last *Fish* type completed but, more importantly, the final conventional freighter built for the company. In 1986 she was temporarily renamed ***ALS Strength*** in connection with a charter but sold the year after to Dimitris Manios (Transman Shipping Enterprises) who renamed her ***Eastman***. Following purchase by Tamahine Shipping in 1989 she was renamed ***Tamathai***. In common with her former Bank Line fleet-mate ***Tamamima***, she was transferred to the Hong Kong register in the early 1990s. In 1995 ***Tamathai*** changed hands again and was renamed ***Clinton K***; in 1997 she was the subject of a further sale and renamed ***Josemaria Escriva*** but remained Hong Kong-flagged. In 1998 yet another change of ownership resulted in the ship's return to the Cyprus register as ***M.P. Trader***. In 2000 she was acquired by another Cypriot company and renamed ***Multi Trader***; pictured at Birkenhead Docks on 25 February 2001. Her bland black funnel was subsequently repainted in a more colourful green and yellow design. For a few years the ***Multi Trader*** had the dubious honour of being the last *Fish* type in service until she arrived at Alang for breaking up in October 2008.

The Shipping Corporation of Saudi Arabia's ***Arab Hind*** (6589gt), seen on 24 June 1995, had a chequered career. She was built by the Burntisland Shipbuilding Co Ltd and in 1965 delivered to Furness, Withy & Co Ltd as the ***Nova Scotia***, registered at Liverpool. In 1973 she was temporarily chartered to Shaw, Savill & Albion Co Ltd for their expanding New Zealand – West coast of South America service and renamed ***Tropic***, but reverted to her former name the following year. A further spell of charter work with Shaw Savill ensued in the mid-1970s, when she was again renamed ***Tropic***. In 1978 she was sold to Booker Line Ltd and renamed ***Booker Valiant***, serving this company until sold to the Saudis in 1980. She was given the name ***Arab Dabbor*** but was renamed ***Arab Hind*** in 1986. She continued in service until sold for breaking up at Alang, where she arrived in March 1998. The small blue mooring boat, about to be lowered by one of ***Arab Hind***'s cranes, deserves an explanation. All ships over 5000gt that use the Suez Canal must carry two mooring boats in a constant state of readiness for lowering, to run ropes to mooring posts or bollards, in the event of an emergency. The boats are hired from the Suez Canal Mooring Company, which also provides a three-man crew required for each one. When ships near completion of transit, the boats are lowered and then steered speedily away to their base.

Between 1969 and 1972 Doxford and Sunderland Shipbuilding & Engineering Co Ltd, Pallion Shipyard, built a class of eight 11408gt (average) aesthetically pleasing freighters fitted with three bipod masts in the forward section, superstructure was located towards the stern. Six of the new ships were delivered to two Greek principals D J Fafalios and Lyras Bros Ltd, one to T & J Harrison Ltd, Liverpool, and one to a Liberian-registered company. Fafalios's ***Finix***, delivered in 1969, was scrapped after almost sixteen years in service but her sisterships fared much better and traded for an average of twenty-eight years. The ***Feax***, completed in 1970 for Fafalios, is seen unladen in Piraeus Roads on 6 September 1985.

Later that year the ***Feax*** was sold to Palmyra Tsiris Lines, placed under the Lebanese flag and renamed ***Parnassus***. By way of contrast the ***Parnassus*** was down to her marks when photographed on 17 June 1994. She was sold to Bangladeshi breakers and arrived at Chittagong in January 1997.

In March 1957 Ghana gained its independence from nearly 140 years of British rule. The new Ghanaian Government was keen to compete against both Elder Dempster Lines and Palm Line Ltd (see page 42), which monopolised the trade between West Africa and the UK. Thus in September 1957 Black Star Line Ltd was formed and granted rights to operate a monthly service between West Africa and the UK. The company flourished and by 1969 owned a fleet of sixteen vessels. The next decade was less fortunate, hindered by Ghana's precarious economic situation and corruption that was rife. Furthermore, Black Star fell behind its rivals in adapting to the increasing use of containers; in a bid to catch up towards the end of the 1970s four identical multi-purpose ships were ordered from Hyundai Heavy Industries, Ulsan, South Korea. The quartet was delivered in 1980, the leading vessel being ***Tano River*** (13304gt). The ***Tano River*** was acquired by a Greek company in 1994, renamed ***Verano*** but registered in Cyprus. She arrived at the River Fal in December 1998 for temporary lay up near the King Harry ferry. She was photographed on 27 February 1999 prior to acquisition by Pacific & Atlantic Corporation, Piraeus, and renamed ***Express Hyphestos*** but remained on the Cypriot register. She retained this identity till arriving at Mumbai in June 2002 for breaking up.

By 1988 Black Star's fleet had dwindled in number to the point that the quartet was its only representatives. In the 1990s all four ships were sold to other owners bringing the company's relatively brief existence to a close in 1998. The last surviving member of the quartet, ***Global Carrier*** (KOR, 13379gt), ex ***World Star***-05, ***Libra Chile***-96, ***World Star***-95, ***Sissili River***-93, was still in service during March 2009. She is seen arriving at Durban in 2005 while briefly registered at Panama following a change of ownership.

(Trevor Jones)

A ship that reaches the age of fifty will almost certainly have done so with a fair bit of luck along the way. A case in point is the freighter ***Sabang*** (1874gt/50) built by C. Van der Giessen & Zonen Scheepswerven N.V., Krimpen a/d IJssel, Netherlands for N.V Koninklijke Paketvaart Maatschappij (KPM); she had two sister ships which were also completed in 1950 but at other Dutch shipyards. The trio was engaged in KPM's Far East services until 1968; the ***Sabang*** was sold to the Ocean Shipping & Enterprises Ltd (OSE) group. During the next decade she was owned by various companies under OSE's control and traded with Panamanian registry throughout using four different names, the last being ***Sea Glory***. In 1981 the ***Sea Glory*** was sold to Birba Navigation S.A., Panama and renamed ***Birba*** but in June the same year ran aground near Kakinada, India. She was abandoned by her crew but subsequently salvaged and taken to Kakinada. After a few months of idleness she was towed to Chittagong, arriving in February 1982, ostensibly for breaking up yet in 1984 was reported still to exist. At some point a Bangladeshi firm acquired her for a new role as a lightening vessel at Chittagong and she was renamed ***Al-Amin***. Fast-forward to 19 November 2001 and the ***Al-Amin*** is seen in the Karnaphuli River, anchored off Chittagong. Amazingly, although appearing battered and scruffy, externally she was much the same as built. She had survived her two sister ships by well over a decade but there has been no further news about this remarkable ship.

In June 2006 the cement carrier ***Katerina. A*** (PAN, 7289gt) joined the exclusive list of exceptional ships to have survived a half-century, a special feat achieved by two distinct phases of equal length. She was completed by Kieler Howaldstwerke A.G., Kiel as the Piraeus-registered freighter ***Orpheus*** for Lyras Brothers Ltd's Panamanian single-ship company Orpheus Marine Transport Corporation. Her construction had been to an extremely high specification for navigation in ice. In 1977 ***Orpheus*** was sold to Maritime Co Esperides S.A., Greece; renamed ***Nireus*** she traded for a further five years as a freighter. The owners of ***Nireus*** decided that she was suitable for specialised cement handling duties after taking into account the ship's superb quality and overall excellent condition. The conversion work was duly carried out at Perama during 1982 and, extraordinarily, her external appearance was virtually unaltered. Her new role, commenced with a three-year contract berthed at Al Haql, Saudi Arabia. In 1986 ***Nireus*** returned to an active career taking cement cargoes to a variety of Mediterranean ports. In 1987 she reverted to a stationary role at Damietta, near Alexandria, Egypt, where she remained until 1991. Incredibly, she again resumed active service as a cement carrier, visiting ports such as Aabenraa, Volos and Liverpool until laid up at Eleusis in 1999. She was subsequently sold to Horus Shipping Co Ltd, renamed ***Katerina. A***, and returned to service in 2000. She was photographed arriving at Alicante on 27 November 2006 and, after self-discharging her cement cargo, sailed for Alang to be broken up. She was beached on the last day of 2006.

The German shipping company Deutsche Dampfscifffahrts-Gesellschaft "Hansa" (more often referred to as D.D.G. Hansa or Hansa Line), formed in 1881, had ordered four ships in the late 1920s with special equipment for the carriage of railway locomotives, wagons and rolling stock. Consequently, these ships, completed between 1929 and 1931, were designed with heavy-lift gear capable of handling loads to 120-tonne, which at the time was an astounding capacity. Unfortunately Hansa's fleet was completely destroyed during World War II thus its commercial services did not re-open until 1950. Thereafter, the company's pre-war experience of carrying heavy loads was developed into specialists in this field. Expertise was gained, not least, by the management's bold decision to fit eight new vessels, completed between 1954 and 1956, with innovative Stülcken derricks devised and patented by shipbuilders H.C. Stülcken Sohn, Hamburg. The Stülcken derrick proved so successful that subsequently nearly all cargo-carrying ships built for Hansa were equipped with one or more. By 1980 Hansa had run into financial difficulties which forced it to file a Deed of Arrangement with the Bremen Court resulting in all its ships having to be sold; a case study is the ***Strahlenfels*** (10644gt/72) built at Lübeck-Siems. She was acquired by Maritime Co. Overseas Inc., Philippines, and renamed ***Zamboanga***. Due to further changes of ownership in 1984 and 1986 she was renamed ***Eastern Express*** (PAN) and ***Kota Ekspres*** (SGP) respectively. In 1994 she was purchased by The Shipping Corporation of Saudi Arabia Ltd and renamed ***Fadel Arab***, pictured on 27 May 1996. She arrived at Mumbai in March 2000 for breaking up.

Between the mid-1950s and early 1960s West German yards built sixteen ships for Hansa Line to designs with the bridge structure placed on the forecastle. This novel feature was devised to obtain maximum possible deck space for heavy-lift cargoes. During the 1970s these ships were sold to various owners (China Ocean Shipping Company acquired nine) and by 1993 nearly all had been scrapped. Among the few survivors was a pair that, ironically, owed their longevity to the container revolution, namely the former ***Wartenfels*** (9724gt/60) and ***Weissenfels*** (9639gt/61). In 1969 the Singapore-based company Neptune Orient Lines had purchased the pair for its northern European or U.S.A. and Middle or Far Eastern services and renamed them ***Neptune Topaz*** and ***Neptune Zircon*** respectively. Towards the end of 1977 it was announced that the pair would be converted into containerships by Ishikawajima-Harima Heavy Industries Ltd, at Aioi, Japan. The work was completed in 1979 and subsequently the ships traded in Asian waters. In the mid 1980s the pair was sold to Bara International Shipping Line Co Ltd, Thailand, becoming ***Supanya*** (the elder vessel) and ***Paithoon*** but in 1993 renamed ***Dragon Bangka*** and ***Dragon Bintan***, respectively. In December 1995 the ***Dragon Bintan*** arrived at Alang to be broken up followed just three months later by the ***Dragon Bangka***, seen at Singapore on 30 December 1995.

The ***Barenfels*** (11801gt/76) was another member of Hansa's fleet when it collapsed due to financial problems. In 1980 she was sold to Prokopiou of Athens, trading as Sea Traders S.A. (see page 46) and with a few strokes of a paintbrush renamed ***Barenbels***. She was photographed on 19 June 1994, by then registered at Malta, carrying an interesting mixed deck cargo between the pair of 100-tonne capacity Stulcken derricks. In 1998 ***Barenbels*** was sold to Ukrainian principals but registered at Panama and renamed ***Kobe Queen I***. The following year she was involved in a rather bizarre matter. She called at Dakar on 3 August 1999 a few weeks after loading about 15000 tonnes of steel in Turkey destined for the Dominican Republic. Later the ship disappeared, with neither owners nor master divulging details of her location, until reported drifting between the Senegalese coast and Cape Verde Islands. On 22 December she was intercepted, under the name ***Gloria Kopp***, off Pondicherry by the Indian Coastguard. After a gun battle she was escorted to Chennai where it was discovered that approximately 2000 tonnes of her cargo had been illegally sold to purchasers in Senegal. Because the owners of ***Kobe Queen I*** allegedly stole the cargo, the ship was seized and eventually auctioned by the Indian authorities. She arrived at Alang for breaking up in February 2002.

Hamburg-Amerika Line's fleet had been decimated by losses during World War II but was rejuvenated by the addition of many fine new freighters built at West German yards during the decade commencing 1951. By the mid-1960s the company, established in 1847, was planning further expansion and ordered seventeen more vessels from various West German shipbuilders. This included a class formed of ten similar ships of 7485gt (average), each completed in 1967, designed for service between north European and West Indies/Caribbean ports. The class nomenclature was West German cities or towns and the ships were well endowed with masts and derricks including a heavy-lift derrick (only two had the Stülcken type). In 1970 Hamburg-Amerika Line and Norddeutscher Lloyd, of Bremen, merged to form Hapag-Lloyd. Nevertheless the ten ships continued in service until sold between 1978 and 1982. China Ocean Shipping Company, which at the time was partial to good quality 1960s European-built vessels made redundant due to containerisation, acquired half a dozen. A Greek operator purchased the Stülcken derrick duo and Lineas Agromar Ltda, Colombia, also bought a pair. Scrapping of the class commenced in 1986. The last two examples, Agromar's ***Corain I***, ex ***Hanau***-79, and ***Corain II***, ex ***Heilbronn***-79, were withdrawn from service in July 1997 and laid up at Barranquilla, Colombia. Both ships are believed to have been broken up prior to 2002. Caribbean and Gulf of Mexico ports had regularly featured in Agromar's schedules; ***Corain II***, minus her heavy-lift derrick, was photographed inward bound for Houston, Texas, on 22 September 1996.

In the late 1960s West German shipbuilders Schiffswerft & Maschinenfabrik Paul Lindenau, Kiel, and Werft Nobiskrug GmbH, Rendsburg, entered into a joint venture to build a series of engine/superstructure all-aft 5000gt freighters known as the *Rendsburg* type. The basic design by Schiffswerft & Maschinenfabrik Paul Lindenau was available with optional extras to meet the requirements of individual owners. However, the majority of the class of more than twenty ships was built by Werft Nobiskrug GmbH, commencing in 1969. Perhaps indicative of the type's high-quality construction is the case of West German-flag ***Jupiter*** (5025gt/69), second ship in the series by Nobiskrug, which in 1979 was renamed ***Jupiter II*** and transferred to Panamanian registry. In June 1985, when entering Londonderry, she collided with a local tug which was badly damaged. In 1986 she returned to the West German register under different ownership and became ***Cap Sunion***. Further changes of ownership in 1989, 1991 and 1995 resulted in her being renamed ***Mandarin Sun*** (VCT), ***Yua Yue*** (CHN) and ***Muhieddine VII*** (HND) respectively. In thick fog one day during the latter part of 1997 she was involved in a collision with the coaster ***Don Ricardo*** (ATG, 1056gt/67) about 13 miles off Kea Island, Greece. The coaster sank without loss of life but damage to ***Muhieddine VII*** was limited to her forepeak. In 1999 she was acquired by the Laila Shipping Co, Syria, and now renamed ***Capt. Abdullah***, she is seen in Istanbul Roads on 27 October 2002. The rendering of her name is debatable; on her bridgeboard it is displayed as ***Captain Abdullah***, which is the version used by *Lloyd's Register*. She was still in service in March 2009.

In 1963 two pairs of handsome new freighters entered service for the Union of Burma Five Star Line, which subsequently became Burma Five Star Corporation. The ***Ava*** and identical ***Bassein*** (each 7435gt) were built by A. G. "Weser" Werk, West Germany, while ***Mergui*** (7458gt) and identical ***Pinya*** (7423gt) were built in Japan by Hitachi Zosen, Osaka, and Uraga Heavy Industries, Yokosuka, respectively. Both pairs of ships were similar except for the heavy-lift cargo handling gear; the German ships were each fitted with a conventional derrick of 100-tonne capacity, whereas a 120-tonne Stülcken derrick was installed in each of the Japanese vessels. For the next two decades the quartet maintained the company's Burma to northern Europe services until made redundant by more modern vessels between 1983 and 1985.

In 1989 Burma Five Star Corporation altered its name to Myanmar Five Star Line after the Burmese military junta passed a law that changed Burma's name to Myanmar; in the same year ***Bassein*** was renamed ***Pathein***. From 1990 the four ships traded exclusively in Asian waters, usually round-trip voyages from Yangon, formerly Rangoon, to Singapore and Bangkok. In 2002 ***Ava*** and ***Mergui*** were renamed ***Inwa*** and ***Myeik*** respectively. 2003 marked the quartet's fortieth anniversary of continuous service for Five Star, a fantastic achievement and a credit to their builders but all four ships' careers were inevitably drawing to a close. ***Myeik*** was sold for breaking up at Yangon near the end of 2003 and ***Pinya*** was withdrawn from service in the second half of 2003. The ***Pathein***'s last reported voyage was in the following year, while ***Inwa*** survived till 2005. The ***Pathein*** and ***Pinya*** are seen at Singapore on 27 June 1998 and 26 June 1999 respectively.

The sister freighters ***Grunwald*** (10188gt/68), ***Westerplatte*** (10188gt/67) and ***Stefan Czarniecki*** (10141gt/67) were notable in Polish Ocean Lines' post Word War II fleet for having been ordered from Danish shipbuilders instead of the customary Polish yards at Gdansk, Gdynia or Szczecin. The ***Grunwald*** and ***Westerplatte*** were an identical pair built by Helsingor Skibsværft, while ***Stefan Czarniecki***, which differed by type of engine, was completed by Nakskov Skibsværft. The three ships were fitted with similar cargo handling gear of a 65-tonne capacity heavy-lift derrick and seventeen other derricks ranging between 5 and 30-tonne capacity. The trio spent virtually the whole of their Polish-flag careers operating between Polish/northern European ports and the principal ports of India, Sri Lanka and Bangladesh, sometimes venturing further east to other countries, for example Australia, Taiwan or Singapore. In 1988 ***Westerplatte*** was sold to Samatour Shipping Co, Egypt and renamed ***Salem Eight***. The ***Salem Eight***, noted sailing from Alexandria on 25 June 1993, was broken up at Alang the following year.

After Communist rule over Poland ended in 1989, the ***Stefan Czarniecki*** was transferred to Polskie Towarzystwo Okretowe S.A., Poland, but was not retained long and arrived at Alang for scrapping in July 1992. The ***Grunwald***, photographed on 26 June 1994, continued in service until sold for breaking up at Alang where she arrived in November 1996.

Between the early 1950s and mid-1970s Danish shipbuilder Helsingor Skibsværft completed more than twenty attractive freighters for the now-defunct firm Ove Skou, of Copenhagen. The majority of these ships were given female Christian names followed by surname *Skou*. This building programme included the ***Dorte Skou*** (9584gt), which introduced a stylish engines/superstructure all-aft arrangement to Skou's fleet in 1968. Seven sister-ships followed, all with Christian names commencing *D*; the final one, ***Dolly Skou*** (9623gt), was completed in 1974. One member of the series, ***Dagny Skou*** (9623gt/71), was extensively damaged by explosions and fire in mid-November 1977. She was subsequently declared a total loss and became the first of the *D*s to leave Skou's fleet when later sold to U.S.A. breakers. Remarkably, she was resold to a Greek company and reconditioned, returning to service during 1980 as ***Pearl Bay***. In 1982 ***Dorte Skou*** and ***Ditte Skou*** (9584gt/69) were renamed ***Jytte Skou*** and ***Benny Skou*** respectively after both were enlarged and radically altered at Yokosuma, Japan. The work included removal and replacement of the vessels' foreparts. Between 1983 and 1984 the remaining *D*s were sold to Singapore or Thailand owners. By the end of 2007 all the unaltered examples of the class were either scrapped or deleted from the registers, except Chinese-flag ***Kai Sheng*** (9589gt/73), ex ***Jutha Malee***-90, ***Diana Skou***-83. The ***Hill*** (LBR), formerly ***Benny Skou***, arrived at Alang for scrapping in October 2008. The ***Rose II*** (PAN), formerly ***Jytte Skou***, was still trading in March 2009. The ***Kai Sheng*** is pictured on 7 May 2005 at Shanghai and an unconfirmed report suggested that she was still active in 2007.

(Author's collection)

Between 1976 and 1978 Helsingor Skibsværft completed a class of five sister ships for Cuba basically modelled on the Skou *D* type but, probably to contain building costs, the quintet were not quite as aesthetically pleasing as their quasi-sisters. Most noticeably the elliptical funnel and graceful cruiser-spoon stern of the *D* type were substituted by a rectangular funnel and transom stern respectively. The leading ship, ***Bolivar*** (9656gt), was delivered to state-owned Empresa Navegacion Mambisa and she set the nomenclature for the class of important or revolutionary former Latin American leaders. In September 1980 ***Bolivar*** was detained at Basra just after the Iran-Iraq war had started and was subsequently declared a total loss. In the 1990s the remaining sister ships continued to be Cuban-controlled even though all were renamed at least once and three of the four transferred to other flags. Between 2001 and 2003 the class was further depleted when three representatives were dispatched to breakers' yards. The last of the type ***Mwafak*** (SLE, 9826gt/77), formerly ***Juarez***, was still active in March 2009. The Cypriot-registered ***Santanita*** (9826gt/77), ex ***San Martin***-90, is pictured sailing from Havana on 26 March 1997. She was sold to unspecified Mongolian-flag interests and renamed ***Anita*** prior to arriving at Sachana for demolition in November 2003.

The 1973 oil crisis caused the market price for oil to quadruple suddenly in 1973/74 and it continued to increase steadily during the decade that followed. This had a huge impact on the cost of operating ships of all types but particularly for high fuel consuming oil-fired steamships. At the time, although the fuel efficient motor ship was the preferred choice of many ship owners, a large number of steam turbine vessels were still in service, many American-owned. One of the prime advantages of turbine units versus diesel engines was savings gained in maintenance but the massive hike in oil prices completely negated any arguments for retaining steam powered vessels. Consequently, ship owners world-wide dispatched their steamers at the earliest opportunity to breakers' yards in China, Pakistan and many other countries. An exception was the United States where for example Lykes Lines continued to operate steam freighters into the 1990s. The ***Jean Lykes*** (11892gt/61) is seen sailing from Liverpool on 9 April 1991. She was renamed ***Velma Lykes*** in 1993 but broken up at Alang in 1994.

(Paul Boot)

Numerous obsolete American-owned steam freighters built in the 1950s and 1960s were not scrapped but instead mothballed in the United States Reserve Fleet, which was already well stocked with World War II-built types including Liberty, Victory and T2 tanker. Occasionally, some of the newer steamships were temporarily reactivated for use in various conflicts such as the Persian Gulf War of 1990/91. Many of the laid up vessels, dubbed "ghost ships", have been scrapped since the start of the new millennium because of environmental issues. Incredibly, the steam-turbine powered freighter ***Cleveland*** (USA, 15949gt/69), managed by Sealift Incorporated, avoided the indignity of long-term lay up and was in service for forty years despite her reputed fuel consumption of 90 tons per day. Her sale to Indian breakers was reported in March 2009 and the following month she was beached at Alang. She was completed as the ***American Mail***, one of a five ship series built by Newport News between 1968 and 1969 for American Mail Line's so called *vagabond* services around the Pacific Rim. Renamed ***President Cleveland*** in 1978, she continued operating in the Pacific trades for American President Lines. In 1989 ***President*** was dropped from her name and Sealift employed ***Cleveland*** for a considerable number of years in the carriage of US aid cargoes to various developing countries, particularly in Africa. This trade often involved a call at Durban for bunkers and victuals; she she is seen arriving at the port in 2005.

(Trevor Jones)

The number of Chinese merchant ships has dramatically increased since the late 1950s by both new and second-hand purchases from abroad, augmented by deliveries from domestic shipyards. In the late 1960s China's principal shipyards located at Shanghai, Dalian and Guangzhou commenced a twelve-year building programme of traditional amidships layout freighters that, paradoxically, coincided with the cessation of constructing this type of ship elsewhere in the world, principally due to the container revolution. Yet it was not until 1973 that the first container services to China commenced on a trial basis operated by Japanese lines; hence the rationale for new conventional vessels. The majority of the new freighters were very similar in appearance and belonged to a group of ships that had names either beginning ***Feng*** (a few ***Da***) or ending ***Yang***. Nearly forty ships built between 1968 and 1980 belonged to this group of 10111gt (average) fitted with three masts and fifteen derricks.The ***Feng Ying*** (9921gt/74) is pictured on the New Waterway inbound for Rotterdam on 2 October 1988. She was delivered to a Chinese breaker's yard prior to 31 May 1999.

(Simon Smith)

In the container-dominated shipping scene of the late 20th century, most surprisingly, the ***Feng***s and ***Yang***s managed to eke out existence as tramp ships pursuing cargoes around the world until the late 1990s, sporadically visiting British and other European ports. However, by the beginning of the new millennium about half the group had been reported scrapped. It has not been possible to establish a definitive number existing in March 2009 but at least three were still active.

After loading a cargo of locally manufactured steel wire, the ***Xin Yang*** (9919gt/75) is seen leaving Cardiff Docks on 29 August 1992. She continued in service for almost five years; in July 1997 she arrived at Alang to be scrapped.

The Soviet Union freighter ***Demyan Bedny*** (10109gt/66), her ownership denoted by the once familiar yellow hammer and sickle on red funnel band, is pictured in the Bosphorus near Istanbul heading for the Black Sea on 20 October 1988. At that time this was considered not particularly remarkable as, every day, numerous Soviet Union-owned vessels used the Bosphorus's busy shipping lanes. Furthermore, Soviet-flag vessels were trading extensively to virtually every part of the globe. Therefore it was almost inconceivable that within just a few years the Soviet Union would collapse into independent nations. Nonetheless, under President Mikhail Gorbachev's leadership major attempts at reform in the Soviet Union introduced in 1986 (perestroika and glasnost), instigated by economic necessity, eventually failed and led to its dissolution. ***Demyan Bedny*** (spelt ***Bednyy*** in the registers), a *Pula* type built in Yugoslavia (see page 58), was among the numerous Soviet merchant vessels which were subsequently transferred to the Ukraine. She was sold in 1997 to unspecified owners and renamed ***Demy*** prior to arriving at Alang for breaking up.

During the 1990s, many former Soviet Union freighters were controlled by Athens-based shipping company, Unimar Maritime Services S.A., via mainly single-ship companies registered in Malta or Panama. Among the medium-sized vessels operated by Unimar was the ***Galina*** (MLT, 4458gt/65), ex ***Voskhod***-91, owned by Galina Maritime Ltd. She belonged to a class of numerous ships built by A. Zhdanov at Leningrad in the 1960s, fitted with three masts and four 5-tonne cranes, a layout well-suited to conveying either containers or bulk cargoes such as timber, coal etc. Interestingly, several of the type were subsequently either transferred to the Soviet Navy or converted into research ships.

The ***Galina*** is seen on 27 June 1995; in the same year she was transferred to another Unimar company Sunset Nav Co Ltd, Malta, and renamed ***Lina M***. In 1997 she was sold to Syrian interests and renamed ***Shaher M***, ultimately arriving at Alang for scrapping in June 2001.

The last two commercially-owned examples were ***Al Bushra*** (SYR, 4645gt/67), ex ***Vasya Alekseyev***-94, and ***Kyrkos*** (4817gt/67), ex ***Ocean Hunter***-97, ***Oka***-95, which in 2003 went to Indian and Turkish breakers respectively. The ***Al Bushra*** was renamed ***Veesham 27*** for her delivery voyage to Sachana and demolition was at an advanced stage when photographed on 23 March 2003.

In November 1996 Unimar Maritime Services S.A. collapsed with debts of several million US dollars. Administrators progressively sold the company's fleet but this was not always a straightforward procedure; this resulted in many of the ships having lengthy periods of idleness. A case in point is the ***Streamer*** (MLT, 4909gt/69), ex ***Pulkovo***-96, which was arrested following the collapse and is pictured languishing in Piraeus Roads on 23 December 1997. She had been built at Vyborg, a Russian port near the Finnish border, and belonged to a class of twenty-three ships delivered to the Soviet Union between the late 1960s and early 1970s which, with one exception, had nomenclature of places in the Soviet Union beginning with *P*. The ***Pamir*** (4540gt/70) was acquired by Unimar in 1991 but following the Soviet Union's demise, all other *P* vessels were transferred to Russian control and operated by either Northern Shipping Company or Sakhalin Shipping Company. By the start of the new millennium half the class had been either scrapped or lost due to casualty. Eventually a buyer was found for ***Streamer*** in 2000 and she was renamed ***Noor Alamal*** under the Cambodian flag. Alas, on 12 April 2002 she sank in the Dardanelles following a collision with the tanker ***Salih Kalkavan*** (TUR, 18829gt/76). In March 2009 the last example, ***Paramushir*** (RUS, 4795gt/71), was still trading in the Far East but by mid-June 2009 she had arrived at Zhangjiagang, China, to be broken up.

The ***Daria I*** (MLT, 4817gt/1968), ex ***Bakaritsa***, also belonged to the Unimar group. She too is seen on 23 December 1997, when in close proximity to ***Streamer***. The ***Daria I*** had arrived at Piraeus from Rostock on 26 November 1996 and was detained for the same reasons as her fleet mate. She was one of five ships built by the Vyborg Shipyard between mid and late 1960s; the quintet was very similar to the class from the A. Zhdanov yard - see ***Galina*** (page 24). The ***Bakaritsa*** had been operated by the Soviet Union's Northern Shipping Company and named after Arkhangelsk's former main port. Her control transferred to Russia after the end of the Communist era. She had been acquired by Unimar's Daria Navigation Ltd only the year before being detained at Piraeus. The ***Daria I*** was less fortunate than ***Streamer*** as a purchaser for further trading was not forthcoming. She was therefore dispatched to breakers at Aliaga, Turkey, where she arrived in June 1998. The last example of the quintet was ***Noor Alddine*** (SYR, 4643gt/1967), ex ***Irina GA***-95, ***Kuloy***-93, which arrived at Mumbai for scrapping in September 2001.

It was Soviet Union convention to assign a project number to each of its new ship designs both naval and merchant; *Project 1563* is more usually known as the *Slavyansk* type, after the leading vessel. A total of thirty-one *Slavyansk* freighters were built by the Kherson Shipyard for the Soviet Union between 1966 and 1973, supplemented by three similar ships built to Soviet plans by Alexandria Shipyard in Egypt. The latter trio, each of 9056gt, was named ***Suez***, ***Ismailiya*** and ***Port Said***, completed in 1973, 1974 and 1975 respectively. The *Slavyansk*'s superstructure was located in the popular three-quarter aft position; subtle variations in the type of cargo gear fitted were found within the class. With the exception of the Egyptian trio, class nomenclature was essentially cities and towns in the Soviet Union beginning with *S*, or prominent Soviet officials. The ***Sochi*** (8874gt/67), named after a Russian city resort, was fitted with ten 5-tonne cranes with open lattice-type jibs. She is seen in the colours of Ukraine's Black Sea Shipping Company (BLASCO) on 1 May 1994 leaving Alexandra Dock, Liverpool, with the assistance of tugs after unloading a cargo of animal feedstuff. In 1997 she was sold to Belize-registered owners and renamed ***Mashraq I*** but it was a relatively temporary arrangement as, in April 1998, she arrived at Alang for breaking up.

In the post-Soviet Union era, 80% of the *Slavyansk* class was transferred to Ukrainian control under the management of BLASCO, while Russia acquired the remaining vessels which were operated by Novorossiysk Shipping Company. The class remained intact until ***General Vladimir Zaimov*** (UKR, 9173gt/73) sank in 1994. Subsequently some ships were sold to other owners and renamed, but between 1996 and 1999 the class was decimated when no fewer than twenty-five members arrived at various breakers' yards in Bangladesh or India. Furthermore, two were deleted from the registers and one was wrecked at Apapa-Lagos. At the start of the new millennium only the ***Svet*** (KHM, 10024gt/70), ex ***Svetlogorsk***-97, and ***Yasmina*** (VCT, 9981gt/1970), ex ***Akademik Yevgeniy Paton***-98, were still in service but both ships were sold to breakers in 2000. The ***Svet*** arrived at Alang in May and ***Yasmina*** at Mumbai in December. One of the Russian ships ***Stoletiye Parizhskoy Kommuny*** (9173gt/71) is pictured on 27 May 1996. She was fitted with a central mast supporting a 60-tonne heavy-lift derrick and six 8-tonne cranes with flat-sided jibs. Paradoxically, this arrangement gave her a more traditional appearance compared with that of the older ***Sochi***. The ***Stoletiye Parizhskoy Kommuny*** arrived at Chittagong for demolition in November 1998.

Between 1968 and 1975 Russian shipbuilder A. Zhdanov Shipyard of Leningrad, named in honour of the city's former party leader, was gainfully employed building thirty-six attractive *Kaliningrad* class freighters, principally for the Soviet Union. Many of those delivered to the Soviet Union were given names commencing "Komsomolets" (meaning a member of the Young Communist League). The class was fitted with either five 8-tonne cranes or one 40-tonne heavy-lift derrick, four 5-tonne derricks and three 8-tonne cranes. Following the Soviet Union's dissolution, the class was transferred in the proportions of two-thirds to the Ukraine and one-third to Russia under the control of Azov Shipping Company and Far Eastern Shipping Company respectively; a number of vessels were subsequently sold to other owners. During the first post-Soviet decade many of the *Kaliningrad* type were dispatched to breakers' yards, mainly in India. In March 2009 ***Rama H*** (GEO, 6168gt/75), ex ***Celmera K***-07, ***Sinjar***-96, ***Komsomolets Turkmenii***-96, was believed to be the last of the type still in service. The Azov Shipping Company's ***Komsomolets*** (UKR, 5923gt/70) is pictured on 18 September 1994. She was sold to other owners in 1996 and renamed ***Ashakrupa*** (VCT); she arrived at Alang to be broken up in July 1999.

Between 1976 and 1982 the Alexandria Shipyard built a series of nine ships for The Egyptian Navigation Company which were very similar to the *Kaliningrad* class. In March 2009 two of the nine were still owned by the company and also in service were ***National Star***, ex ***0015 May***-00, and ***Haj Khalil*** (SYR, 6160gt/79), ex ***Ahmos***-01. The ***Haj Khalil*** is seen in Limassol Roads on 25 May 2003.

The Soviet Union's *Projects 1585* and *1585E* are both better known as the multi-purpose freighter *Dnepr* type.The name *Dnepr* is a mutation of the River Dniepr (sometimes spelt *Dnipro*) at the mouth of which Kherson is located in southern Ukraine. Between 1972 and 1985 a total of forty-six *Dnepr* vessels, which included thirty-one for export customers, were built by the Kherson Shipyard. The type's popularity was underlined when two vessels were delivered to the famous Ocean Group (Blue Funnel Line) in 1976. All *Dnepr* ships were fitted with a 63-tonne heavy-lift derrick and seven 12-tonne cranes, sufficient to handle a variety of cargoes such as containers, grain and timber. Pictured at Singapore on 17 June 1999 is ***Kapitan Petko Voivoda*** (11750gt/74), one of a half-dozen examples of the type completed for Navigation Maritime Bulgare, Bulgaria. The ***Kapitan Petko Voivoda*** was distinguished for being the first export example to be delivered and uncommonly retained the same name throughout her career. After spending most of 2002 laid up at Varna, on the Bulgarian Black Sea Coast, she arrived at Sachana for scrapping in December 2002.

More than a decade after the completion of ***Kapitan Petko Voivoda***, the last *Dnepr* built, ***Otto Parellada*** (12030gt/85), was delivered to Empresa Navegacion Mambisa, Cuba. However, she spent most of the 1990s trading under the Cypriot-flag as ***Evgenisos***, ***Adamas Pearl***, ***Prima*** and ***Caprice*** in that order. The ***Caprice*** is pictured sailing from Swansea on 9 May 2000 after discharging a cargo of Brazilian hardwood; in the same year she became the ***Irazu*** (VCT). In 2004 she was renamed ***Eastern Carrier*** (KOR) and, in March 2009, was one of only nine *Dnepr* vessels confirmed as still in service.

The fifteen *Dnepr*s built for the Soviet Union were augmented by two second-hand purchases in 1986. The Soviet Union's dissolution resulted in the transfer of all seventeen vessels to the Ukraine, of which fifteen were controlled by the Black Sea Shipping Company (BLASCO) and two by Azov Shipping Company. A common alteration made to the ships, often towards the end of their careers, was removal of the heavy-lift derrick. At first glance the Ukrainian-controlled ***Hurst*** (BHS, 11854gt/80), ex-***Grigoriy Petrenko***-97, seen at Singapore 18 June 1997, seems to be a case in point. However, her derrick had been set in an unusual lowered position as not required while the ship was idle. She was under arrest and had been inactive for a lengthy period in respect of matters involving BLASCO. Intriguingly, it is believed ***Hurst*** was named after an England football player as were four other Ukrainian ships ***Pearce***, ***Shearer***, ***Sheringham*** and ***Southgate***, all managed by Silver Line/V Ships. Subsequently in 1997 the ***Hurst*** was renamed ***Lucy*** and transferred to the St. Vincent & Grenadines flag, but remained under Ukrainian control until sold, at a relatively young age, for breaking up at Alang where she arrived in September 1998.

The ***Lucy*** was among the first batch of *Dnepr* ships to be scrapped and in the next decade many more were broken up at Alang too. The last *Dnepr* built for the Soviet Union was ***Ivan Pereverzev*** (12030gt/84) operated by Azov Shipping Company. The company's Ukrainian management eventually changed her name to ***Shakhtar*** in 2001, but two years later she was acquired by Commercial Fleet of Donbass LLC, Mariupol. She is seen arriving at Durban in 2006 and was still trading during March 2009.

(Trevor Jones)

In 1960 Polish shipbuilder Stocznia Gdanska, Gdansk completed the first of sixteen *B514* type freighters for the Soviet Union, which were purposely designed to convey timber in bulk. The type had an ice-breaking bow, midships bridge/accommodation, three bipod masts and ten derricks including one of 40-tonne lifting capacity. The *B514*s were given names ending "les", meaning timber in Russian. They typically traded to northern European ports with timber cargoes from Baltic ports but could carry other bulk commodities such as coal or grain. Many *B514*s had been scrapped by the time the Soviet Union was dissolved. In 1997 the ***Komiles*** (4720gt/60), owned by Joint Stock Shipping Co Prisco Traffic Ltd, Russia, became the last *B514* in service; in the same year she was sold to another Russian concern, Fortuna Tanker, and renamed ***Fortanles***. On 14 December 2000 she arrived at Singapore and remained idle there for some time. In 2001 she was renamed ***Forta*** after being sold to unspecified Cambodian-flag interests. She was photographed at Singapore on 24 March 2001 during the course of raising her port bow anchor immediately before sailing for Alang to be broken up.

Between 1963 and 1967 the Polish *B44* type and very similar *B44/1* type formed a class of thirty freighters delivered to the Soviet Union by Stocznia Gdanska and Stocznia Szczecinska respectively. These types were designed with superstructure/engines positioned three-quarters aft, a popular arrangement at the time, and fitted with four bipod masts, a 60-tonne derrick, eight 10-tonne and four 5-tonne derricks. The leading *B44*, ***Murom*** (9695gt/63), set the naming theme of places chiefly in the Soviet Union beginning with M, though nine vessels were named in honour of prominent writers, for example Tolstoy. Scrapping of the class commenced in the late 1980s; at the end of the Soviet Union era two-thirds remained, of which more than a dozen vessels were transferred to Ukrainian control, but demolitions steadily continued in the 1990s. 1996 was a particularly black year when eleven members arrived at various breakers' yards and one more was wrecked at Mumbai. The last example in service, ***Sea Bee*** (VUT, 9598gt/67), ex ***Boris Lavrenyov***-96, arrived at Chittagong to be broken up in June 1997. It is worth mentioning that the *B44/1* type should not be confused with the *B441* type, which was subsequently marketed as the Polish Liberty Ship Replacement design, though very few were ever built. The *B44* type ***Romen Rollan*** (UKR, 9714gt/67) was photographed on 27 June 1995; she arrived at Alang to broken up in May the following year.

Traditional amidships layout freighters had become uncommon visitors to European waters by the mid-1990s. It was therefore a treat to photograph standard Polish *B41* type ***Smolny*** (8718gt/68) on 23 June 1994, as it was in October 1995 when she made her last call at a U.K. port, Immingham. She had a collection of eighteen derricks including one of 50-tonne lifting capacity. In the decade commencing 1964, all *B41*s were delivered by Stocznia im Komuny Paryskiej at Gdynia with the exception of a pair by Stocznia Szczecinska, Szczecin. Interestingly, the construction of the hulls for the latter pair, ***Piotr Dunin*** (8650gt/66) and ***Josef Wybicki*** (8644gt/67) was subcontracted to Spanish yard Ast de Cadiz, at Seville. Similarly, the hulls of a second pair, ***Major Sucharski*** (8756gt/74) and ***Marian Buczek*** (8839gt/74) were built at the Lisnave yard in Lisbon before being fitted out by Stocznia im Komuny Paryskiej. The ***Smolny*** was one of thirteen *B41* vessels delivered to Polish Ocean Lines. Also, China, Albania and the French company Messageries Maritimes took delivery of five, one and one ships of the type respectively. Thus there were twenty vessels in the series. The ***Smolny*** served POL very respectably for more than 25 years. In 1994, without change of name, she was acquired by Euroeast Lines S.A. & Heneage Maritime Inc, Liberia, managed by Martec S.A., of Luxembourg. She is pictured in Euroeast colours and continued in service for a few more years until sold to breakers at Alang where she arrived in May 1996.

Within the *B41* class several non-standard versions evolved with design changes made to the superstructure, cargo gear or other minor details. The ***Marian Buczek*** (8839gt/74) is an example of one of these ships. Her modifications included the fitting of a 60-tonne Stülcken derrick instead of a conventional heavy-lift derrick, and superstructure fully extended to hull width. By coincidence, she was photographed exactly a year to the day after ***Smolny***. The many ships of this size owned by POL were affectionately known by the company's staff as "tenners", being of about 10000dwt. Between 1979 and 1984 serious casualties resulted in POL unfortunately losing three of its *B41* ships. Furthermore, the Chinese-owned ***Jiu Yi Shan*** (8496gt/69), ex ***Hai Ning***-92, sank in 1995. Remarkably, the career path of the ***Marian Buczek*** closely resembled that of ***Smolny***'s. She served POL for twenty years, was transferred to Euroeast in 1994 and finally sold for breaking up in 1997. She was renamed ***Marian*** before arriving at Alang in November the same year. In March 2009 the continued existence of China's four remaining *B41* vessels was very much in doubt.

Between 1967 and 1975 Stocznia Szczecinska built eighteen *B445* type freighters, the majority for Polish Ocean Lines. The class was designed with an unusually small funnel, raised hull level beneath superstructure, tapering to the poop. It is noteworthy that Stocznia Szczecinska's *B478* and *B474* types, built in the mid-1970s, were similar to the standard *B445*. Ironically the last *B445* completed, the ***Iran Gheyam*** (IRN, 8408gt/75), ex ***Arya Rooz***-80, was the first of the type to be withdrawn from service following shelling and fire damage at Khorramshahr in October 1980 during the Iran-Iraq war. Scrapping of the class commenced in the mid-1980s and by the start of the new millennium only Iran Shipping Lines' ***Eco Elham*** (8027gt/74), ex ***Iran Elham***-96, ***Arya Kish***-80, and ***Eco Ekram*** (8027gt/74), ex ***Iran Ekram***-96, ***Arya Rokh***-80, were still in service. The pair was scrapped by Indian breakers in 2002. Following the end of Communist rule over Poland in 1989, POL was radically restructured involving privatisation of its operational divisions, and by 1996 six new companies had been formed. Pictured on 24 September 1994 is POL-Seal's well laden ***Wladyslaw Jagiello*** (8309gt/71); POL-Seal had been established earlier in 1994 as part of the privatisation process. The ***Wladyslaw Jagiello***, named after the king of Poland who reigned from 1386 to 1434, continued in service until sold to breakers at Alang, where she arrived in December 1997. It should be added that several *B445* ships, launched for POL in the late 1960s, were completed for other owners, including one named ***Wladyslaw Jagiello*** which became the Shipping Corporation of India's ***Vishva Vikas*** (8422gt/68).

The Polish *B40* and *B40/1* types were built by Stocznia Gdanska and Stocznia Szczecinska respectively for the Soviet Union between 1968 and 1970. Both types formed a class of twenty near-identical freighters. The whole class except for one vessel was operated by the Black Sea Shipping Company (BLASCO), Odessa, on world-wide tramping duties. After the Soviet Union was dissolved jurisdiction of BLASCO transferred to the Ukraine and its fleet adopted the rather bland funnel colour of white with black top. A few of the company's vessels were subsequently acquired by other Ukrainian operators that used alternative funnel colours for example the Ukrainian Shipping Company (USC). The whole class was scrapped between 1996 and 2000, the majority by Indian breakers. One of the last examples was USC's ***Ignatiy Sergeyev*** (10028gt/68), photographed on 20 September 1994, which was demolished at Kakinada in 2000 after being beached and abandoned there following a collision with a local dredger in 1996.

Ho Chi Minh (9941gt/70) was the sole member of the *B40* and *B40/1* types operated by Far Eastern Shipping Company (FESCO), Vladivostok (see ***Ignatiy Sergeyev***, page 35). In common with her sister ships she was used in the world-wide tramping trades. Following dissolution of the Soviet Union, control of FESCO passed to the Russian Federation. In September 1992 the company's legal status was changed and the state enterprise transferred to Far Eastern Shipping Company PLC. The company's ships adopted funnel colours of white with a white F partially bordered in red on a blue band.

The ***Ho Chi Minh*** was named after the revolutionary and statesman born in 1890 who served as president of North Vietnam from 1946 to 1969, in keeping with the class's mainly prominent-Communists' nomenclature. She is pictured, minus her 60-tonne Stülcken derrick, while taking on bunkers in Piraeus Roads on 23 December 1997. The following year she was sold to Cambodian-flag interests, renamed ***Nina***, and arrived at Alang for breaking up in early June 1999.

The elegant Polish *B442* type freighter, designed during an era when the container ship revolution was still in its infancy, was basically a development of the *B44* and *B44/1* types (page 31). Stocznia Gdanska at Gdansk built a series of nine *B442*s between 1968 and 1972. The class's principal features included superstructure and machinery located three-quarters aft; cargo gear consisted of a 60 or 65-tonne Stülcken derrick and sixteen 5-tonne derricks. The leading ship, ***Konin*** (10063gt), was delivered to Polish Ocean Lines. She operated in POL's services between Poland and northern European ports to the Middle and Far East. The ***Konin*** is seen on 19 September 1994 carrying an unusual deck cargo, perhaps drilling equipment, and remarkably part of the structure hangs over the hull just forward of the Stülcken derrick. Earlier in 1994 she had been acquired by Euroeast Lines S.A. & Heneage Maritime Inc, Liberia. She arrived at Alang for scrapping in April 1996.

Interestingly, four *B442* ships were delivered to the Turkish State company D.B. Deniz Nakliyati T.A.S., established in 1955. The quartet's nomenclature was distinguished Turkish military generals, for example ***General K. Orbay*** (10240gt/70), launched as ***Turuszon***, in honour of Kazim Orbay who served as Chief of the General Staff of the Turkish armed forces between 1944 and 1946. The quartet faithfully served the company for more than a quarter-century in the worldwide general cargo trades, and in particular between Turkish and Far Eastern or U.S.A. ports. However, the ***General A.F. Cebesoy*** (10058gt/69), launched as ***Swiecie***, suffered a serious engine-room fire on 2 April 1998 and was subsequently scrapped at Aliaga, Turkey. During 2000, the year D.B. Deniz Nakliyati was privatised, the remaining trio were all sold for breaking up at Alang; the ***General K. Orbay***, pictured on 26 June 1994, was renamed ***General K. Orbay 2*** prior to arriving there in June.

Very near the end of her career, Chinese-owned freighter ***Su Xia*** (10009gt/71), made an impressive sight in Manila Bay on 18 June 1998; her hatch covers had been opened preparatory for cargo discharge at Manila. The ***Su Xia*** was built as ***Lucjan Szenwald***, owned by Polish Ocean Lines and subsequently the Chinese-Polish Joint Stock Shipping Company. Co-operation between China and Poland had started in 1951, under a bilateral agreement forged between the governments of the two countries, when Soviet Russia instructed Poland to support an arms shipment to the Communist Chinese armies in the Far East and Korea. Moreover, the Nationalist Chinese attempt to blockade mainland ports, resulting in the seizure and confiscation of two Polish and one Russian ship in 1954, brought further cooperation between Poland and Communist China, which eventually led to a formal ownership arrangement in 1977 known as the Chinese-Polish Joint Stock Shipping Company. The ***Lucjan Szenwald***, named after a 20th century Polish poet, was officially designated a *B442* but deviated markedly in outward appearance from the standard design. She had modified superstructure, a streamlined funnel and a raised deck aft. The ***Wladyslaw Orkan*** (POL, 10120gt/71) was virtually an identical sister ship. In 1986 ***Lucjan Szenwald*** was acquired by China Ocean Shipping Company's regional subsidiary Jiangsu Shipping Company, China, and renamed ***Su Xia***. At some point her 60-tonne Stülcken derrick was removed. Prior to arriving at Alang for breaking up in early October 1998, she had been transferred to the St. Vincent & the Grenadines flag. In 1987 the ***Wladyslaw Orkan*** was also acquired by China and renamed ***Yan An Wu Hao***. By March 2009 her continued existence was very much in doubt. Therefore, perhaps, the last *B442* type was ***Swiecie*** (LBR, 9847gt/71). After a long lay up at Gdynia, during which time she was first renamed ***Ramada*** (PAN) and later ***Ramada I***, she arrived at Liepaja, Latvia, for scrapping in September 2002.

Between 1968 and 1971 a series of eight *B446* type freighters of 6575gt (average) was completed by Stocznia Szczecinska, Poland. Six were delivered to Polish Ocean Lines, which had been established in 1951, and a pair to China Ocean Shipping Company. The *B446* had sleek lines, a heavily raked-back funnel and streamlined superstructure which all contributed to a unique futuristic appearance. Leading vessel ***Zakopane*** introduced POL's naming theme for its *B446* ships of Polish towns or cities commencing Za. The new ships supplemented POL's substantial fleet of freighters involved in regular shipping services worldwide. Unfortunately, the second in the series ***Zamosc*** (1969) became a total loss after a collision with another vessel in January 1979. The five *B446* ships were transferred to some of the new companies formed in the post-1989 restructuring of POL; for instance ***Zawiercie*** (1970) came into the ownership of Polskie Towarzystwo Okretowe S.A. She is seen in Piraeus Roads on 22 June 1993 but soon afterwards commenced her delivery voyage for demolition and arrived at Alang in August 1993. The ***Zakopane*** was sold to other owners in 1993, renamed ***Pearl I*** (VCT) and broken up in 1997. In 1996 ***Zabrze*** (1969) was sold to a Syrian owner and renamed ***Alfarah 1***; she was broken up at Alang in 2001. ***Zawichost*** (1970) and ***Zambrow*** (1969) were scrapped in 1997 and 1998 respectively. The last reported activity of the Chinese pair, ***Feng Cheng*** and ***Yan Cheng***, completed in 1971, was in 1998 and their continued existence is very doubtful. Therefore, the last *B446* in service may have been ***Alfarah 1***.

Between 1972 and 1976 Polish shipyards Stocznia Gdanska and Stocznia Szczecinska built thirty-five *B46* type freighters for the Soviet Union, of which a significant number were registered with the Estonian Shipping Co (ESCO), Tallinn. The class nomenclature was prominent Communist officials. In August 1991 Estonia regained its independence from the Soviet Union and the following month ESCO was transferred to the Republic of Estonia. By mid-December 1991 ESCO had been reorganized into a state-owned company (it was fully privatised in 1999) and its fleet adopted new white/blue/black funnel colours. All ESCO's *B46* vessels were hastily renamed after Estonian towns and villages, for example the ***Andrey Andreyev*** (6555gt/73) became ***Kunda.*** She is pictured on 25 September 1994 well-filled with a cargo of timber. About half of the *B46* ships were broken up in the 1990s and the remaining survivors before 2004. The ***Kunda*** was acquired by Amberg Maritime Ltd, Malta, in 1995 and renamed ***Amber II***. She arrived at Alang for demolition in November 2000.

The *B46* was equipped with a useful range of cargo gear which consisted of one 60-tonne Stülcken derrick, six 10-tonne derricks, two 5-tonne derricks and two 8-tonne cranes. The hull dimensions were comparable to those of the Liberty type ships and therefore suitable for accessing many ports of the world. The ***Vestaurus*** (BRB, 6876gt/73), ex ***Loksa***-95, ***Vasiliy Shelgunov***-92, is pictured sailing from Newport, Gwent, on 25 August 1996 after unloading a full cargo of animal feed. Her appearance is in sharp contrast to that of ***Kunda***. Conspicuously absent are her Stülcken derrick and one of the two 8-tonne cranes, while much rust covers her hull. In 1997 ***Vestaurus*** was sold to Conto Lux Inc under the St Vincent & the Grenadines flag and she was renamed ***Helena S***. Perhaps not surprisingly, she was delivered to Indian breakers at Alang in September the following year; beforehand her name had been tweaked to ***Nals***.

(Author's photo, courtesy of Capt. Danny Lynch)

In the early 1970s conveyance of containers by sea was rapidly developing as many shipping companies world-wide added specialised container ships to their fleets. Nevertheless, the UK-West Africa route, although not immune to the spread of containerisation, still traded a good deal of commodities suited to more conventional ships. Elder Dempster Lines Ltd, its West African connections dating back to 1852, operated a sizeable fleet of pre-mid 1960s-built freighters which were not particularly well-suited to the container age. Thus, with an urgent need to replace tonnage, Elder Dempster acquired a pair of Polish *B430* type multi-purpose vessels named ***Shonga*** (9236gt/73) and ***Sherbro*** (9239gt/74). The pair was a radical departure from the company's other vessels, not least by having engines and superstructure all located aft. Between 1976 and 1979 a third *B430*, the ***Monsun*** (9049gt/73), was chartered from a West German owner, and for the duration renamed ***Sapele***.The former ***Sherbro*** is pictured on 27 June 1997 as the Singapore-registered ***Meng Yang*** at her home port. She had been sold by Elder Dempster to a Liberian company in 1984 and renamed ***Sherry***, going on to acquire a long list of names through various further sales and charters. She was finally renamed ***Fong Dar*** not long before arriving at Alang to be broken up in March 1998. The career of the ***Shonga*** followed a similar path; she was scrapped at Guangzhou, China, in 1997.

The ***Echo Pioneer*** (BHS, 9691gt/81), ex ***EAL Sapphire***-90, ***Costa Rica***-89, is pictured sailing from Swansea on a sunny 24 September 2000 after discharging a cargo of hardwood from Brazil. She was the twelfth and final Polish *B430* type built by Stocznia Szczecinska. Ships of this series completed in the latter part of the 1970s differed from those built before, such as ***Meng Yang***, by not having a pair of masts and derrick in front of the superstructure. It is noteworthy that Elder Dempster Lines added three more *B430* ships to its fleet between 1979 and 1980, albeit by leasing, which emphasised how eminently suitable the type was for its UK-West African services. This was chiefly due to the ships' large twin hatchways, lower holds, 'tween decks without sides and overall dimensions compatible for navigation in West Africa's mangrove swamp areas with soft mud banks, known as Creeks. The ***Echo Pioneer*** was sold to Syrian interests and renamed ***Abeer S*** in 2002; two years later she was purchased by Lily Enterprises Pvt. Ltd, Maldives, and became the ***Lily Crown***. In March 2009 the only *B430* vessels still in service were ***Lily Crown***, ***Krokus*** (MLT, 9696gt/79), formerly ***Guatemala***, and ***Bulk Trader*** (PAN 9475gt/80), formerly ***Sapele***.

Between 1973 and 1979 Stocznia Szczecinska built a series of *B432* type freighters of 5487gt (average) for Polish Ocean Lines (POL), Federal Arab Maritime Co, Egypt and Syro-Jordanian Shipping Co, Syria which took delivery of eight, three and two ships of the type respectively. In July 1990 POL's ***Skoczow*** (1977) sank due to a collision with another vessel. The ***Wieliczka*** (1973) is seen in Limassol Roads on 20 June 1993; she was sold in 1999 and renamed ***Wise Mariner*** (MLT) prior to arriving at Mumbai for demolition. Between 2000 and 2008 four more Polish-owned *B432* ships were broken up. Meanwhile ***Siemiatycze*** and ***Bochnia***, both built in 1976, were sold to Panamanian owners and renamed ***Tiran Island*** and ***Rabbana*** in 2001 and 2006 respectively. In December 2008 the ***Rabbana*** was beached at Mumbai for scrapping and three months later ***Tiran Island*** arrived at Sachana for breaking up.

The Egyptian-flag vessels, all completed in 1978, were sold to other owners. The ***Al Hamraa*** was acquired by Muhieddine Shipping Company, Syria, in 1996 and renamed ***Haj Muhieddine***, pictured on 24 June 2001 off Tartous, Syria's principal port. She appears to be exceptionally well cared for, but nonetheless her sale to Indian breakers was either imminent or had already happened, as just over six weeks later she arrived at Alang. The ***Al Esraa*** and ***Asmaa*** were both sold to other Egyptian owners in 1993 and 1999 respectively. ***Al Esraa***, renamed ***Trans Cargo III***, was still in service in March 2009. ***Asmaa*** became ***Transmar III***, but in 2006 was renamed ***Transmar*** and scrapped at Alang in 2007. The 1979-built Syrian-owned ***Al Yarmouk*** and ***Barada***, remarkably having retained their original names, were still in service during March 2009.

Stocznia Szczecinska also built a reefer version of the *B432* type. The thirteen-ship series was delivered to the Soviet Union between 1978 and 1981 and assigned to fish-carrying duties. After the Soviet Union's demise all were transferred to the Russian Federation and subsequently owned by Stock Shipping Co "Vostotransflot". Scrapping commenced in 1997 and by the end of 1999 seven vessels had been delivered to Indian breakers' yards, including ***Igen Wave*** (BOL, 5801gt/81), ex ***Kutuzovo***-99, at Mumbai. She is seen on 29 December 1999 just four days after having been beached. In February 2000 the ***Igen Faith*** (5816gt/79), ex ***Trunovsk***-99, arrived at Mumbai also for scrapping. Chinese breakers purchased three more of the type between 2002 and 2003.

Only two examples were sold to other owners for further trading. The ***Talniki*** was acquired by Ukrainian owners in 1999 and renamed ***Seapride*** (5816gt/80), pictured at Singapore 31 March 2002. She subsequently became ***Sea Ranger*** (PRK), then ***Karema*** (COM) and finally ***Rock*** (SLE) prior to being broken up at Gadani Beach in 2007. The ***Kulikovo*** became the Panamanian-registered ***Zabrjad*** (5795gt/81) in 2002. Her demolition at Mumbai after beaching in February 2009 rendered the *B432* type reefer extinct.

In the 1980s a series of eleven *B181* type multi-purpose ships, essentially a larger version of the *B430* (see ***Echo Pioneer***, page 42), was built by Stocznia Szczecinska for various owners including former well-known British shipping firm Palm Line. The ninth *B181* completed, ***MSC Cristiana*** (PAN, 17700gt/84) was photographed 23 May 2004 off Battery Point, Portishead, shortly before docking at Portbury, Bristol. She was making one of her last voyages in original guise before being converted into a dedicated container ship by removal of the impressive masts and Hallen-type derricks. She had been delivered to West German owner H Schuldt as ***Euro Star***. During the course of her career she was renamed no fewer than nine times, indicative of spells on charter to various shipping lines as well as changes in ownership. The initials MSC stand for Mediterranean Shipping Company S.A., based at Geneva, which was founded in 1970 and has since grown at a spectacular rate to become one of the largest container shipping lines in the world. The ***Karine*** (PAN, 16564gt/81), delivered as ***Medi Star***, and ***Patriot*** (IND, 17702gt/83), formerly ***Toledo***, were both scrapped at Alang in 2003 and 2007 respectively. Nine B181 vessels were still in service during March 2009 but soon afterwards four more were sold for demolition including the ***MSC Cristiana*** which was beached at Alang on 9 July 2009.

In 1971 the P&O group underwent a major reorganisation, which resulted in merging the activities of over one hundred subsidiary companies into five operating divisions. The new P&O General Cargo Division (GCD) took over the cargo liner trades previously worked by the likes of P&O Lines, Federal Steam, Moss Hutchinson and many more. The GCD, which became P&O Strath Services Ltd in 1977, embarked on gradually rationalising and reducing its fleet but there was also a requirement to replace a number of its older ships. Hence six identical freighters with container capacity and fitted with a huge 300-tonne Stülcken derrick were ordered from the Stocznia Gdanska shipyard. These ships, known as the *B466* type, were all delivered between 1977and 1979 but had very short careers with P&O being replaced by container ships in the early 1980s. Five out of the six vessels were sold to various Greek companies all managed by Sea Traders S.A. Remarkably, between 1988 and 1993 the quintet was acquired by the Islamic Republic of Iran Shipping Lines and given names beginning "Iran", for example ***Iran Mahallati***. Amazingly all five ships, each of 13914gt, have continued in service with Iran Shipping. However, between October 2008 and March 2009, four were renamed as part of the fleet nomenclature changes to dispense with "Iran", which commenced in 2007. Consequently, ***Iran Broojerdi*** (1978) formerly ***Strathelgin***, ***Iran Kolahdooz*** (1977) formerly ***Stratheden***, ***Iran Baghaei*** (1979) formerly ***Stratherrol***, and ***Iran Bagheri*** (1978) formerly ***Strathesk***, were renamed ***Dinna***, ***Despina***, ***Kijea*** and ***Danoosh*** respectively. The ***Iran Mahallati*** (1978), ex ***Lindenbels***-88, ***Strathewe***-83, was photographed on 19 June 1994. It has not been possible to establish if she has a new name too.

The ***Floreana*** made an imposing photographic subject at Singapore on 26 June 1999, when she paused for bunkering purposes during a voyage from Laem Chabang, Thailand, to the Port of Bristol, with a cargo of hardwood. Her prominent black funnel, with two white bands close together, is a nostalgic reminder of the British India Steam Navigation Co Ltd, which was acquired by P&O in 1914, but finally lost its identity following P&O's major reorganisation in 1971. The ***Floreana*** had been completed as ***Isla Floreana*** (12677gt). She and sister ship ***Isla Salango*** (12676gt) were a unique pair of Polish *B345* type freighters built by Stocznia Gdanska in 1979 for TRANSNAVE, Ecuador. The hull and superstructure design was very similar to P&O's *B466* type (see ***Iran Mahallati***, page 46). In 1997 the pair was acquired by Mauritius-flag interests and, rather lethargically, renamed ***Floreana*** and ***Salango***.

Later in 1999 ***Floreana*** was sold to Gulf Breeze Ltd, Cambodia, managed by Kaalbye Shipping Ukraine KSU and renamed ***Zarina III***. In 2000 ***Salango*** was renamed ***Prospects*** by her owner and transferred to Indian registry. In 2003 ***Zarina III*** transferred to the St. Vincent & the Grenadines flag, and in the same year ***Prospects*** was scrapped at Chittagong. Finally, ***Zarina III*** was sold to breakers at Alang, where she arrived in April 2006. She is seen sailing from Durban on 10 October 2005.

(Trevor Jones)

On 5 February 1999 the ***POL Daisy*** (VUT, 13251gt/82), ex ***Indian Express***-98, ***Kriti Jade***-89, one of eight Polish *B346* type freighters built by Stocznia Gdanska between 1981 and 1984, grounded in the Eastham Channel, River Mersey, with a full cargo of steel. A major disaster was avoided when the ship was refloated some hours later; nonetheless, the incident was to seal her fate. The ***POL Daisy*** subsequently sailed from Ellesmere Port, via the Tyne, for Gdynia where she arrived on 22 February 1999. Initial reports by Lloyd's suggested that she was at Gdynia 'for repairs' but this was subsequently altered to 'awaiting repairs'. Despite this encouraging news, ***POL Daisy*** remained at Gdynia for nearly four years with little or no work undertaken. Eventually she was sold for breaking up and after being made seaworthy sailed from Gdynia as the North Korean-flagged ***Veesham 24*** in December 2002. She was beached at Sachana on 22 March 2003 and photographed the following day.

The *B346* leading vessel ***Nawabshah*** (12080gt), owned by Pakistan National Shipping Corporation (PNSC), sank after grounding off Rondo Island in 1985. In March 2009 the ***Thor Mercury*** (THA, 13251gt/1984), formerly ***Kriti Peridot***, was beached for demolition at Mumbai and PNSC's ***Sibi*** (13402gt/81) arrived at Gadani Beach, Pakistan, to be scrapped. She is seen at Dunkirk on 22 May 2006. In March 2009 also ***Thor Merchant*** (THA, 13251gt/1982), formerly ***Kriti Amethyst***, made a delivery voyage to Chittagong breakers and beached the following month. Thus, at 31 March 2009, the *B346*s still in commercial service were PNSC's ***Khairpur*** (13402gt/81) and the 13251gt Thai-flagged pair ***Thor Mariner*** (1983) and ***Thor Master*** (1982) formerly ***Kriti Garnet*** and ***Kriti Coral*** respectively.

(Simon Smith)

Between 1963 and 1967 VEB Schiffswerft 'Neptun', Rostock, was engaged in building its third major series for the Soviet Union known as the *Povonets* type. The class of forty freighters was designed with superstructure located two-thirds aft. Nomenclature was predominantly places in the Soviet Union. Ships of this design were regularly noted at ports throughout Europe until the 1990s, when the majority were sold by their post-Soviet Union era owners to various other principals before being scrapped. The ***Rima M*** (SYR, 3237gt/65), ex ***Stepans Halturins***-96, ***Stepan Khalturin***-91, is pictured on 16 August 1997 in Cawsand Bay, Cornwall, waiting to enter Plymouth Docks to discharge a cargo of bagged fertiliser. She was formerly named after an important person in the Russian revolutionary movement of the late 1870s who had founded the Northern Union of Russian Workers (thus one of the few exceptions in the naming theme). In 1999 ***Rima M*** was renamed ***Riad M*** but on 26 June 2000 she suffered a serious engine-room fire off Cyprus and was towed to a Syrian port; repairs were completed in 2001. She was subsequently sold to unspecified Sao Tome & Principe-flag interests and renamed ***Dana*** but in August the same year a second major fire destroyed her accommodation. ***Dana***'s crew of fifteen was rescued but an aerial search made afterwards failed to locate the ship, which was presumed to have sunk. In March 2009 it was believed the Vietnamese-owned pair ***Baikal 01*** and ***Baikal 02*** (both 3354gt/66), formerly ***Shilka*** and ***Svirsk*** respectively, were still active in the Far East but the continued existence of four more examples was doubtful.

VEB Schiffswerft 'Neptun' built thirty-two *Pioner* type freighters for the Soviet Union between 1968 and 1972. The *Pioner* is essentially a development of the *Povonets* type; notably the *Pioner's* breadth is three feet greater, its bridge height reduced by one deck level and superstructure top deck extended to full length of the accommodation area. In May 1972 the ***Grisha Akopyan*** (3411gt/69) was severely damaged by an American air attack at Cua Ong and subsequently scrapped at Hong Kong. The ***Nina Sagaydak*** (3601gt/70) became the second *Pioner* major casualty in October 1983 after being crushed by ice, and sank near Kosa Dvukh Pilotov in the Soviet eastern Arctic. After the Soviet Union was dissolved all thirty surviving examples were transferred to Russian control. With the exception of several ships, the type was allocated in equal proportions between the Far Eastern Shipping Company and the Murmansk Shipping Company. Later some vessels were sold or transferred to other owners. Scrapping commenced in the mid-1990s. In March 2009 only six were known to be still in service and the continued existence of another three was doubtful. After passing beneath the Severn Bridge, the Belize-registered ***Tolya Komar*** (3718gt/71) was photographed on 19 July 1997 off Beachley, bound for Sharpness, with a cargo of bagged fertiliser. Subsequently, in the same year, she became the ***Mickael M*** (VCT) and in 1999 ***Mareg II*** (GEO) but there has been no further news about her since she sailed from Mombasa in January 1999.

The name *Pioner* was chosen as a tribute to the Young Pioneer organization of the Soviet Union, which had been founded in 1922 and was the Soviet Union equivalent of the Scouts movement. Another example, the ***Pavlik Larishkin*** (RUS, 3693gt/71), is pictured on 21 March 2002 making good progress in the New Waterway towards Rotterdam. The distinction of retaining this name through her long career came to an end in 2006 when she was acquired by St Kitts & Nevis-flag owners and renamed ***Bader T***. She was still in service during March 2009.

(Author's collection)

The East German shipyard VEB Warnowwerft at Warnemünde, a district of Rostock, constructed vessels chiefly for other Soviet Bloc countries and China. Between 1963 and 1968 the yard completed a series of eighteen 9500gt freighters for the Soviet Union, known as the *Vyborg* type after the leading ship (the naming theme being Russian places commencing with the letter V). Other export customers included a Norwegian owner and the China Ocean Shipping Company. The class had distinctive features which included substantial three-quarters aft bridge/accommodation, three bipod masts in the forward section and a raised deck aft. Many of the Soviet Union *Vyborg* vessels were broken up in the two or three years either side of its dissolution. One of the exceptions was ***Vostochnyy*** (9455gt/68). In 1992 she came under the control of Unimar Maritime Services S.A. (see pages 24 and 25), owned by Martina Holding Corporation, and was renamed ***United Victory*** (HND). The following year she loaded pumice in Greece destined for Barry, the penultimate shipment of this material to the Welsh port, and, after discharging the cargo, is pictured departing on 27 April 1993. Unimar's sudden demise in November 1996 resulted in her arrest the same month at St. Nazaire, France. Eventually she was sold to unspecified Cambodian-flag interests and renamed ***Victoria***. She arrived at Calcutta for scrapping in March 1998 and had the honour of being the last former Soviet *Vyborg*. The last active *Vyborg*, Chinese-flag ***Xing Long*** (9513gt/68), ex ***Hai Men***-92, was reported at Hong Kong in September 1999, but her continued existence is very doubtful.

Many of VEB Warnowwerft's principal standard freighter types which followed the *Vyborg* were fitted with a distinctive form of heavy-lift derrick, comprising two vertical posts each of which carried a cantilevered outrigger platform to achieve the necessary separation of the span guys. Pictured on 23 June 1994 is a splendid image of a 60-tonne version of this striking arrangement, as fitted in *Rostock* type ***Lady Bana*** (HND, 8501gt/67), ex ***Eilenborg***-93, ***Eilenburg***-91. VEB Warnowwerft built a total of sixteen examples of this type between 1967 and 1970 all of which were delivered to Deutsche Seereederei, East Germany. The *Rostock* ships were named after East German towns and cities ending in "burg", with the exception of leading vessel ***Rostock*** (8501gt). Approximately ten years after the reunification of East and West Germany in 1990, the whole class had been scrapped. The ***Lady Bana*** arrived at Alang in December 2000.

The VEB Warnowwerft building programme for the Soviet Union included a series of a dozen similar-sized freighters, known as *Type 17*, which were all completed between 1968 and 1970. The *Type 17* was installed with a set of eight 5-tonne cranes, resembling some of the *Slavyansk* type, such as ***Sochi*** (see page 26). The leading vessel ***Irkutsk*** (9352gt) was named after a city in Siberia but the class nomenclature was divided equally between places in the Soviet Union and names commencing *Akademik* or *Professor*. The Soviet Union's demise brought the *Type 17*s under the control of either Russia or Ukraine, operated by Baltic Shipping Company or Black Sea Shipping Company (BLASCO) respectively. However, the days of this type were numbered and scrapping commenced in 1993, although a few were subsequently acquired by other owners. In May 1999 the ***Phoenician Trader*** (PAN, 9373gt/70), ex ***Professor Nikolay Baranskiy***, arrived at Calcutta for demolition which rendered the class extinct. The ***Irkutsk*** is seen in BLASCO colours at Singapore on 30 December 1995 just six months before she arrived at Alang for demolition.

Between 1970 and 1972 VEB Warnowwerft built fourteen *Type 17b* freighters which were similar to the *Type 17*s except for cargo gear arrangements. The *Type 17b* was typically fitted with a builder's trademark heavy-lift derrick of 60-tonne capacity, four 8-tonne derricks and six 5-tonne cranes. A few ships were given the last name "Ulyanov" to honour certain relatives of Vladimir Lenin (born Vladimir Ulyanov). After the Soviet Union's collapse the whole series was operated by the Baltic Shipping Company, Russia. The ***Valerian Kuybyshev*** (9323gt/71) is pictured on 21 June 1995 and appeared to be reasonably well cared for. In 1996 the Baltic Shipping Company was declared bankrupt. Consequently, in 1997 ***Valerian Kuybyshev*** was acquired by Euroshipping A/O, Russia and renamed ***Euroshipping 6***. She arrived at Alang for scrapping in January 1999. The *Type 176* was consigned to the history books in 2001 after Bangladeshi breakers at Chittagong demolished ***Un Dok-1*** (PRK, 9323gt/72), ex ***Nikolay Tulpin***-96.

During the 1990s the financial situation of Romanian state-run shipping company NAVROM seriously deteriorated culminating in its bankruptcy and appointment of a liquidator in 1999. Consequently a number of its ships were arrested or detained at ports around the world, for example ***Focsani*** (10046gt/76) at Manila. The ***Focsani*** had arrived at the Philippines' principal port in 1996 from India and is pictured languishing in Manila Bay on 18 June 1998. She is an example of an *Ozean* type freighter, essentially an improvement of the *Rostock* type, of which forty were built by Warnowwerft between 1970 and 1980. Typically, *Ozean* ships were fitted with a 70-tonne heavy-lift derrick and sixteen 10-tonne derricks. There were, however, some noticeable variations in the cargo gear and appearance of the superstructure within the class. Ten of the class were delivered to China Ocean Shipping Company. Another major customer was the Scindia Steam Navigation Company, India, which in the early 1970s took delivery of eight ships fitted with bipod masts. The ***Focsani*** was due to be auctioned in April 1999 and departed from Manila prior to 11 February 2000 but her exact fate has not been established. Her continued existence is considered extremely doubtful along with three of the Chinese ships, ***Hong Men*** (10058gt/75), ***Yi Men*** (10173gt/78) and ***Yu Qiang*** (9672gt/1974), ex ***Tian Men***-93, which have had no movements reported since the late 1990s.

The final *Ozean* type completed was NAVROM's ***Panciu*** (9544gt/1980). Between 1997 and 2004 she traded under various guises, including reverting at times to ***Panciu*** and illegally as ***Ciuta*** during 2002/3 on the West African coast. In June 2004 she sailed from Freetown for Tema in dubious circumstances but the subsequent history of this vessel is a complete mystery. Scrapping of the *Ozean* ships commenced in the mid-1980s and by 2003 thirty-two had been delivered to various breakers' yards or deleted from the registers. The class number was further reduced by three ships which foundered because of accidents or stormy weather. Thus ***Panciu*** was, perhaps, the last of the type in service. She is seen as the ***Lady Doris*** (BLZ) in Limassol Roads on 1 June 2002.

The isolated town of Mongla, Bangladesh, is approximately 80 kilometres inland from the Bay of Bengal, situated at the vast confluence of the Pussur and Mongla rivers. The Port of Mongla has limited shore facilities which are supplemented by anchorages in the Pussur River for goods to be loaded or unloaded using ships' gear. The Shipping Corporation of India's ***Vishva Kaumudi*** (IND, 11001gt/80) had been idle at the port for over 2½ years when photographed in the anchorage area on 22 November 2001. She had brought a cargo of rice to Mongla but, due to a dispute between her charterers and owners over the cargo, it was about eight months later before discharge began. Her situation worsened when subsequently placed under arrest by the consignees. In 2002 she was reported sold to the Six Star Corporation, Bangladesh. The ship eventually sailed in tow from Mongla on 1 May 2003 for Chittagong to be broken up. The ***Vishva Kaumudi*** was one of the numerous *Meridian* type ships built by VEB Warnowwerft in the 1970s and early 1980s for various owners. This type was a notch-up on the *Ozean* design, being slightly longer, five feet beamier and with a greater heavy-lift capacity. Six *Meridian* ships were confirmed as still in existence during March 2009. The type moved closer to extinction when two vessels arrived for demolition at Gadani Beach in May 2009. The noted survivors were ***Ataqa*** (PAN), ***Ha Na*** (PRK), ***Markovo*** (RUS) and ***Sea Star*** (KNA), formerly ***Schwerin***, ***Potsdam***, ***Jalamurugan*** and ***Tivat*** respectively.

The last major series of ships that VEB Schiffswerft 'Neptun' delivered to the Soviet Union was a 4500gt multi-purpose class. A total of nineteen ships named after places in the Soviet Union, the majority beginning with the letter R, were completed between 1973 and 1976. The type was designed to carry a relatively small number of containers; cargo gear fitted consisted of a 40-tonne derrick and three 20-tonne derricks. Following the Soviet Union's demise, the control of many of these vessels transferred to Ukrainian Danube Shipping Company. In the decade or so afterwards, several vessels were sold to other owners and renamed, while casualties or demolitions took their toll. Thus, in March 2009, only about half of the original number remained. The ***Reutov*** (UKR, 4966gt/75) is seen on 24 June 1996 entering Durban with an unusual mixed deck cargo of containers, trucks and trailers. She was sold to Turkish ship breakers at Aliaga in 2008.

VEB Warnowwerft's ultimate series of large freighters was the multi-purpose *Monsun* type. The class of fifteen ships was completed between 1979 and 1985 for various export customers with the exception of ***Radebeul*** (13557gt/84), which was delivered to VEB Deutfract/Seereederei, Rostock. The *Monsun* was designed basically as an updated and slightly larger version of the *Meridian* type. Notable features include bridge/accommodation and machinery positioned all aft, container capacity for 523TEUs and a heavy-lift derrick capable of handling 125-tonne loads. The three-quarter bow angle of ***Theofano*** (CYP, 13430gt/82), ex ***Presidente Ibanez***-94, ***Wangoni***-83, pictured at Marina Di Ravenna, Italy, on 20 September 1998, illustrates her sturdy cargo gear mounted well above main deck level to facilitate handling containers. In 2006 she was sold to Hong Kong (China)-flag interests and renamed ***Flotec***.

In March 2009 almost all the *Monsun* vessels remained in service with the exception of leading vessel ***Hamilton*** (BHS, 13521gt/79), ex ***Grigoriy Kozintsev***-97, ***Faneos***-86, which had a relatively short life of twenty years. She arrived at Alang for scrapping in December 1999. However, the ***Ever Star*** (PAN, 12811gt/84), formerly ***Wadai***, arrived for demolition at Chittagong on 24 May 2009. The ***Kety II*** (PAN, 12811gt/82), formerly ***Wahehe***, makes a fine sight at Durban on 23 September 2008. It is noteworthy that at some point her heavy-lift derrick was removed. In 2009 she became the North Korean-registered ***Kuk San***.

(Trevor Jones)

The Federal People's Republic of Yugoslavia did not rely as heavily on the Soviet Union for shipbuilding work as Poland and East Germany. Nevertheless, Yugoslavian shipyards constructed a considerable number of vessels for the Soviet Union, particularly in the 1960s and 1970s. The "Uljanik" yard on the Bay of Pula, one of the oldest shipbuilders in the world, participated in this work and between 1964 and 1971 built a series of twenty handsome freighters of the superstructure three-quarter aft type. The series was divided equally into two groups, which differed only marginally. The leading ship of the first group was appropriately named ***Pula*** (10109gt). She was fitted with three bipod masts, a pair of kingposts towards the stern and a total of fourteen derricks including two of 60-tonne lifting capacity. In 1991 she was acquired by Katran Shipping Company Ltd, Honduras and renamed ***Astra***, pictured on 27 May 1996. Alas, six months later she was delivered to Bangladeshi breakers at Chittagong.

The ***Nazym Khikmet*** (10109gt/65), in common with sister ship ***Astra***, belonged to the first group of the *Uljanik* type. All the members of this group were owned by the Soviet Union's Black Sea Shipping Company (BLASCO), Odessa. With the exception of ***Pula***, both the first and second groups' nomenclature was writers, poets and critics. The ***Nazym Khikmet***, named after the Turkish author and talented poet who shared Communist views, is pictured arriving at Avonmouth 5 December 1992 after BLASCO had been transferred to Ukrainian control. The soft lighting conditions were perfect to accentuate her pleasing lines. She brought a cargo of animal feed from India. This was a regular trade at the port until it started to be conveyed in larger ships, and from different sources such as South America, to new facilities at Portbury a few years later. The ten ships of the first group were sold for demolition between 1993 and 1998; ***Nazym Khikmet*** survived until February 1997 when she was delivered to M R Enterprises at Chittagong.

In 1913 the port of Barry exported just over 11 million tons of coal, a world record, which constituted one eighth of the total exports of both coal and coke from the British Isles. After World War I ended, the trade went into gradual decline. By the 1980s Barry made only occasional exports of coke which completely ceased in mid-1986. During the early 1990s Barry Docks briefly handled coal shipments again but, ironically, imports conveyed in former Soviet Union ships usually of under 5000gt. It was, therefore, a surprise when the ***United Might*** (MLT, 10204gt/69), ex ***Gavriil Derzhavin***-91, owned by Far Eastern Shipping Co (Malta) Ltd, brought a full cargo of coal to the port from the Ukraine; she was photographed berthed in No. 2 Dock on 22 January 1994. The ***United Might*** belonged to the second group of the *Uljanik* class and it is worthy of note that four of the type were converted to carry containers. Nine out of the ten members of the second group were sold for demolition in the 1990s, including ***United Might*** to Chinese breakers just a few months after her visit to Barry. The last one was Far Eastern Shipping Company's container vessel ***Gamzat Tsadasa*** (RUS, 13212gt/71), which remarkably survived until December 2008 when she was beached at Alang for demolition.

A further series of ten freighters, similar to both the *Uljanik* groups, was built by Brodogradiliste "III Maj", Rijeka, between 1967 and 1970 for the Far Eastern Shipping Company (FESCO). The leading ship was named ***Dubrovnik*** (10152gt), after the historic Yugoslavian city, but the rest followed the *Uljanik* groups' predominant writer or poet nomenclature. In the post-Soviet Union era, Russian-controlled FESCO retained the 10152gt trio ***Nikolay Karamzim*** (1969), ***Sergey Yesenin*** (1968) and ***Vladimir Mayakovskiy*** (1968) until they were sold for breaking up in the mid-1990s. Meanwhile the other members of the series were renamed after transfer to either Maltese or Honduran registered companies during the early 1990s. The ***Dubrovnik*** temporarily traded as ***Daphne*** before being scrapped in 1992, and five of her sister ships were broken up between 1994 and 1999. At the start of the new millennium ***Hanuman*** (VCT, 10835/70), ex ***Lester Lynx***-99, ***U. Alexander***-97, ***Aleksandr Vermishev***-92, was the sole example. She was demolished at Mumbai in 2001. The ***United Glory*** (MLT, 10152/69), ex ***Makhtum-Kuli***-91, was actually on her way to Alang for demolition when photographed on 25 June 1995.

The ***Opatija*** (9746gt/73) belonged to a family of eleven similar freighters built by Brodogradiliste "III Maj" between the late 1960s and 1977 for Cuban and Yugoslav principals. Some vessels of this type were fitted with goalpost masts as an alternative to single masts. The ***Opatija*** was delivered to Jugoslavenska Linijska Plovidba (JLP), Yugoslavia, established in 1947. Within the post-World War II Communist-governed Yugoslavia, Croatia was one of the constitutive federal republics. In 1991, Croatia proclaimed independence and in 1992 it was recognized by the United Nations; thus in the same year JLP changed its name to Croatia Line. The company's distinctive livery had been unmistakedly applied to ***Opatija*** when photographed on 16 June 1994. Confusingly, perhaps, her registered owner was Cross Seas Shipping Corporation, St. Vincent & the Grenadines. She was delivered to breakers at Alang in July 1997.

The ***Dunlin*** (BLZ, 10379gt/77), ex ***Vivian***-99, ***Pine Islands***-98, ***Arieto***-96, ***Aracelio Iglesias***-90, is seen sailing from Havana on 26 March 1999. Astonishingly, the pilot was already in the course of disembarking even though his charge had only moments before cleared the narrow channel leading to the port. She was one of three freighters built by Brodogradiliste "III Maj" in 1977 for the Cuban state shipping company Empresa De Navegacion, Mambisa. The trio belonged to the same family as ***Opatija*** but fitted with goalpost masts. Nomenclature was important black Cuban Communist leaders of the 1930s, such as Aracelio Iglesias who was leader of the dock workers. The ***Dunlin*** has a dark green colour scheme which was applied to many Cuban controlled ships using various free flags for example Cyprus and Malta. She was later registered at Malta before being sold to breakers at Alang, where she arrived in September 2001. The last example of this type ***Jin Kun*** (PRK, 10379gt/77), formerly ***Jesus Menendez***, has not had any movements reported since December 2007.

Between the late 1960s and early 1970s, the O/Y Wärtsilä A/B shipyard at Turku built a fine class of freighter for the Soviet Union known as the *N* type. The class of fifteen vessels was named after towns or cities beginning *Novo*. Principal features included superstructure well set-back from midships and five 5-tonne cranes. Following Soviet Union dissolution, control of the *N* type was transferred to Russia and the ships operated by Baltic Shipping Company (BSC). The bankruptcy of BSC in 1996 maybe hastened the demise of the type as the majority of the class was subsequently acquired by various owners and renamed before being dispatched to breakers at either Alang or Chittagong. By the start of the new millennium only three survived. However, one of the trio, ***Sibirsk*** (KHM, 8802gt/67), ex ***Novosibirsk***-97, arrived at Alang in January 2000. ***Novomoskovsk*** (RUS, 9493gt/67) was the last of the type. She was renamed ***Novo*** for a delivery voyage to breakers, arriving at Alang in May 2005 after having spent almost a decade idle and under arrest at Ibiquy, Argentina. The ***Wald Al-Agouz*** (9465gt/69), ex ***Novopolotsk***-97, was the last *N* type in commercial service. She is pictured in the Karachi outer anchorage on 23 December 2000 not long after having transferred from the United Arab Emirates to Cambodian flag. In 2001 she was renamed ***Al-Agouz*** before delivery to Indian breakers in August the same year.

The scale of the Soviet Union's forest products industry may be put into perspective by the huge number of specialist timber-carrying ships that were added to its fleet in the 1960s and early 1970s. Finnish shipbuilders alone delivered seventy vessels of the type with superstructure positioned two-thirds aft and generally fitted with three bipod masts, eight 5-tonne and a single 35-tonne capacity derricks. Some vessels had an unconventional Hallen mast with a mixture of cranes and derricks. In their heyday regular trading patterns included carrying timber cargoes from the Baltic Sea region to northern European ports, but, when not required in the timber trades, could convey bulk commodities such as grain or wheat. A splendid example of the type fitted with a Hallen mast is ***Alhareth*** (SYR, 2778gt/63), ex ***Uniprogress***-96, ***Kungurles***-94, built by Hollming Oy, Rauma. She is pictured on 26 June 2001 off Tartous. Although ***Alhareth*** (or ***Al Hareth*** in the registers), was seemingly very well cared for by owner Ahemt Abdulkader Fahl, in January 2003 her demolition commenced at Mumbai, India.

Only a few Finnish-built timber ships of the superstructure two-thirds aft type were scrapped in the 1980s. The rest were transferred to several of the Soviet Union's succeeding independent nations, notably Lithuania and Russia, but were approaching the end of their useful lives and not retained for long. Nonetheless, some Mediterranean-based operators, especially, appreciated their versatile qualities. A case in point is the ***Kimry*** (2723gt/69), built by Hollming Oy, Rauma, which was disposed of by the Baltic Shipping Company, Russia in 1996 to St Vincent & Grenadines-flag interests and renamed ***Hindo***. In the same year she was transferred to a Syrian owner. She appeared immaculate when photographed on 17 June 2001 anchored off Beirut. In 2002 she became the Cambodian-flagged ***Josmar*** and finally was sold to breakers at Mumbai in 2004.

Surprisingly, about sixty of these timber carriers were still active at the commencement of the new millennium but, during the next decade, a substantial number were scrapped and a few became casualties. Thus, in March 2009 it was believed that nineteen were still active. In the following two months, however, Chinese breakers claimed a further six vessels, which left the type coming perilously close to extinction. The final ship of the type, ***Kedaynyay*** (2723gt), was delivered by Hollming Oy in December 1971. After the end of the Soviet Union she was transferred to the Lithuanian Shipping Company and renamed ***Kedainiai*** and she is seen as such in the River Severn after sailing from Sharpness on 13 June 1996. In 1998 she became the Cambodian-flagged ***Captain Ahmad*** and continued in service until sold to Indian breakers at Mukalla where she arrived in September 2003.

Between 1961 and 1964 a series of a dozen Soviet Union timber carriers was built by Valmet OY, Finland with fully aft bridge/accommodation. The ***Igarkales*** (2730gt/62) and ***Permjles*** (2872gt/63) were both scrapped at Gadani Beach in 1988. The Soviet Union's dissolution resulted in the transfer of the ***Irbitles*** (2731gt/62) to Latvia (she was renamed ***Seda***) and her nine sister ships were transferred to Russian control. By the mid-1990s all these vessels had been disposed of to other owners and re-registered at ports in countries such as Malta and Syria. This brought about a major change in their trading patterns, which shifted from Baltic Sea/Northern Europe regions to the warmer climes of Black and Mediterranean Seas. In March 2009 ***Makkia*** (SYR, 2714gt/64), formerly ***Istra***, seemed to have survived but her last reported movement was in 2004. The ***Samara-S*** (SYR, 2703gt/62), ex ***Sinar***-00, ***Moustafa S***-96, ***Unistar***-94, ***Inkurles***-91, photographed off Tartous on 28 June 2001, was in service for more than forty years. She was broken up at Alang in 2004.

The ***Kros Istanbul*** (KHM, 2812gt/63), ex ***Furkan***-02, ***Shaher M***-96, ***Blaze***-95, ***Izhevskles***-93, seen in Istanbul Roads for bunkering purposes on 21 June 2003, was also in service for more than forty years. She was sold in 2004 to K M S Enterprises, Cambodia and renamed ***Gnocchi***. In 2006 she was simply renamed ***Occhi*** before delivery for scrapping at Aliaga in September of the same year. Therefore she may have been the ultimate example of the type.

From the late 1950s Romania ceased to be under direct military and economic control of the Soviet Union. Nonetheless, both countries maintained close ties until the Romanian Revolution of 1989. Consequently, Romania, in common with other Eastern Bloc countries, benefited from the Soviet Union's huge requirement for new ships chiefly in the 1960s and 1970s. The Santierul Naval shipyard at Galatz gained some of this work, which included building a series of twenty-two identical small freighters. Attractive vessels, they were constructed between 1967 and 1970 to plans of a class built mainly in the mid 1960s by Soviet yards. Their design made them well-suited for the timber trades; essential features included an ice-breaking bow, three bipod masts, and eight 5-tonne and one 15-tonne derricks. The majority of these Romanian-built ships were named after places in the Soviet Union beginning with *K*. Following Soviet Union dissolution, one-third of the series was transferred to Azov Shipping Co, Ukraine, including the ***Kustanay*** (3041gt/69) seen in Piraeus Roads on 23 December 1997. In 1998 she was sold to Shehadah Maritime Company Ltd and became ***Noor El Moustafa*** under the Cambodian flag. In 2001 she was acquired by Silver Seas Shipping Services and renamed ***Hassan*** without change of flag. In 2006 she was sold to Rose Trading S.A., St. Kitts & Nevis flag, and renamed ***Narjes***. The ***Narjes*** was noted lying in Piraeus Roads at the end of December 2008 but the following month made her final voyage to Mumbai. On 28 February 2009 she was beached for breaking up. Only two of the type, ***Krasnopolye*** (RUS, 3041gt/68) and ***Imperatorskaya Gavan*** (KHM, 3041gt/1968), ex ***Katangli***-00, were believed to be still trading during March 2009, both based in the Far East.

The Japanese *Freedom* type, designed with all-aft engine/superstructure and three goalpost masts, strongly rivalled the *SD14* design in the highly competitive Liberty Ship Replacement building programme. The *Freedom*, which has very similar principal dimensions to the *SD14*, was developed by Ishawajima-Harima-Heavy Industries (IHI) shipyards, unusually, in conjunction with a Canadian firm, G.T.R. Campbell (International) Ltd. The *Freedom* has the distinction of being the first of all the worldwide Replacement designs to be put into production. Between 1967 and 1979 the IHI yards built an impressive number of more than one-hundred and twenty vessels, while a few more were built under licence in other countries, principally Singapore. These ships were particularly popular with owners operating under the Greek and Liberian flags, which accounted for approximately one hundred of the total completed. The *Freedom*'s basic design, unlike the *SD14*, was not developed further by a series of upgrades, although some ships differed by having greater derrick capacity. Many *Freedom* ships have been scrapped, although several were noted by enthusiasts at European ports during 2008. In March 2009 the ***Radnor*** (CYP, 8953gt/75) ex ***Alegre***-94, ***Telfair Lady***-86, ***Hermina***-80, visited London with a cargo of sugar. A fine example is ***Turan. C*** (TUR, 9145gt/74), ex ***Makron***-00, ***Saronikos***-94, ***Fair Winds***-89, ***Oakland***-85, photographed at Istanbul on 29 October 2003. In the following year she was transferred to the Panamanian flag. She arrived at Mumbai for breaking up in April 2009.

Arguably the *SD14*, designed by Austin & Pickersgill Ltd, Sunderland, is the most famous and successful of the various Liberty Ship Replacement types which were marketed worldwide by shipbuilders commencing in the second half of the 1960s. The four series of the *SD14* design and the *SD14* variants formed an impressive total of two hundred and eleven ships built between 1968 and 1988, the majority at British yards. *SD14* design work commenced in 1966, yet more than four decades later about 25% of the total vessels built were still in existence. The photogenic qualities of the *SD14* design may be appreciated by this splendid 2005 view of ***Saigon 3*** (VNM, 9011gt/1980), ex ***Scotian Express***-93, ***Jade II***-87, arriving at Durban in boisterous conditions. In 2008 she was renamed ***Golden Light***.

Throughout this lengthy period, Durban has been one of the few ports that *SD14*s have frequently visited in the general cargo trades and for bunkering or dry-docking purposes. The year after the previous photograph, the ***QSM Dubai*** (PAN 9213gt/1978), ex-***Tania***-06, ***Empros***-03, received a general overhaul and repainting. When photographed afterwards she appeared in fine fettle.

(both Trevor Jones)

A perfect autumn day encouraged many *SD14* admirers to make a special effort to witness ***Lady Steel*** arriving in the River Mersey, for it had been a long while since one of the type had docked at a British port. The ***Lady Steel*** (PAN, 8976gt/81), a Brazilian-built *SD14* variant, was completed as ***Lloyd Argentina*** for the once-famous Brazilian company Lloyd Brasileiro, which ceased trading in the 1990s. ***Lloyd Argentina*** was sold to another Brazilian owner in 1989; a string of subsequent sales to various owners followed in the 1990s and in 2002 she notched up her sixth name, ***Lady Steel***. She is seen on 18 October 2003 part laden, coincidentally, with a cargo of steel and shortly before turning in the river to enter Birkenhead Docks.

Almost a year later the ***Lady Steel*** was sold yet again and renamed ***Gaspard***, retaining Panamanian registry. This proved to be a short-term arrangement as, in 2006, she was renamed ***Dalia I*** and then ***Nordana***, following two more sales both involving Panamanian-flag interests. She was still in service during March 2009. The ***Gaspard*** is pictured at Durban soon after having acquired her new identity.

(Trevor Jones)

Many of the *SD14* vessels still in service during March 2009 were controlled by China or North Korea and operated by subsidiary companies, usually in the Far Eastern trades only. During the first decade of the new millennium, a few British ship enthusiasts made regular visits to Shanghai. They had their endeavours and patience well rewarded by sightings of several veteran *SD14*s, including a few active in the Chinese coal trades only. The prime location for viewing shipping movements at Shanghai is the famous tourist spot at the heart of the city named the Bund, which stretches one mile along the banks of the Huangpu River. However, at Shanghai (which in 2006 became the world's busiest port by cargo tonnage) the sheer number of barges or small vessels using the river is sometimes a nuisance when trying to photograph a particular ship. A good solution to this issue is to stay in one of the nearby hotels, and when checking in, ask for a room near the top overlooking the river.

From an elevated position two *SD14s* inward bound on the Huangpu River are pictured in 2006. The Brazilian-built ***Fortune Sea*** (PAN, 9328gt/79), formerly ***Monte Alto***, passes the Bund on 24 April. By contrast in the lower photograph taken on 2 November the ***Jin Da Hai*** (CHN, 8859gt/76), formerly ***Ormos***, built by Austin & Pickersgill Ltd, was carrying a full cargo of coal.

(Author's collection)

Although the *SD14* proved highly successful for Austin & Pickersgill, their *SD14* derivative designs *SD9*, *SD12*, *SD15* and *SD18*, disappointingly, drew little interest from ship owners. However, there was enthusiasm among a few Brazilian ship owners, including Lloyd Brasileiro, for a modified version of the *SD15* which was marketed as the 11372gt *Prinasa-121*. This resulted in CCN shipbuilders, Rio de Janeiro, completing a series of thirteen of the type between 1975 and 1982; five were fitted with masts and derricks, eight had deck cranes. Between the late 1980s and mid-1990s many *Prinasa* vessels were sold to either Far Eastern or Mediterranean-based owners for further trading and subsequently scrapped. In March 2009 only the identical 1980s-built ***Long Fu*** (PAN) and ***Man Pung*** (PRK), formerly ***Frotamanila*** and ***Frotasingapore*** respectively, remained in service. The ***Amar*** (SGP), formerly ***Frotadurban***, was believed to be laid up off Pulau Batam following a serious fire incident on 16 August 2006. The ***Long Fu*** was photographed at Ko Sichang, Thailand, on 27 June 2006 shortly before she commenced loading cargo by means of conveyor from local barges.

Austin & Pickersgill's *SD18* multi-purpose freighter was designed with superstructure and engines-aft, a container capacity of nearly 500 TEU and six Velle swinging derricks capable of handling loads up to 55 tonnes. Despite these features only three vessels of the type were ever ordered, all by the Pakistan National Shipping Corporation (PNSC) in 1979. Construction was completed in 1981; the 11940gt ships were named ***Muree***, ***Kaghan*** and ***Ayubia***. In October 1989 the ***Muree*** sank twenty miles off the coast of Devon in hurricane conditions. Fortunately, her two sisters served PNSC for many more years and had fairly uneventful careers trading mainly between Karachi, Europe, the Middle-East, Japan or south-east Asia. The ***Kaghan*** is seen on 20 September 1994 carrying a considerable number of containers on deck.

In contrast to the ***Kaghan***, the ***Ayubia*** was completely empty, her future uncertain, while laid up in Karachi's outer anchorage on 23 December 2000. Both ships were scrapped at Gadani Beach in 2004 and 2001 respectively.

West German shipyards were also highly prominent in developing and marketing Liberty Replacement types. Moreover, the designs known as the *German Liberty*, *36* and *36L*, were particularly successful because, similar to the *SD14*, many optional alternatives or additions to the basic versions were available to satisfy individual requirements of ship owners. In the decade commencing 1968 in excess of one hundred ships of these three types were built, the majority for export customers. The Flensburg-built ***Mannan*** (MLT, 9278gt/73), ex ***Rizcun Hong Kong***-88, ***Pitria Star***-80, is a splendid example of a *German Liberty* type. She is seen in Karachi's outer anchorage on Christmas Day 2000; her conventional bow and unsophisticated cargo handling gear are conspicuous. ***Mannan*** arrived at Alang to be broken up in July the following year.

The *German Liberty* was designed by a consortium of shipbuilders comprising Bremer Vulkan, Flensburger Schiffsbau-Gesellschaft and Rickmers Werft. The substantially prefabricated vessels were constructed at their Vegesack, Flensburg and Bremerhaven yards respectively. The Bremer Vulkan-built Chinese-owned ***Hua Mao 12*** (8959gt/69), formerly ***Maria Oldendorff***, is pictured passing the Bund in Shanghai on 31 March 2004; her foremast remains but she has been stripped of all other gear for the coal trades. In 2007 she was renamed ***Hua Mao 16*** and was still in service during March 2009.

(Simon Smith)

The West German Liberty Replacement types *36* and *36L*, designed by AG Weser and built at its Seebeck Shipyard, Bremerhaven, were developments of its original version type *36* (of which only a few were built). All these types were basically similar to the *German Liberty*, but the type *36* (improved version) and type *36L* were built with a bulbous bow. An example of the improved version of type *36* is the ***Sheng Yuan*** (9631gt), seen in Manila Bay on 21 June 1998, which was fitted with an interesting range of cargo handling gear. She was completed in 1974 as the ***Adam Asnyk*** owned by Polish Ocean Lines and subsequently the Chinese-Polish Joint Stock Shipping Company, (see page 39). In 1991 she was acquired by China Ocean Shipping Company, allocated to its regional subsidiary Liaoning Steam Shipping Company and became the ***Sheng Yuan***. It is believed she was renamed ***Chang Ming*** in 1999 but with certainty prior to 2004. In July 2005 she was transferred to Dalian Jin Heng Shipping and renamed ***Jin Tai Hai***. In 2007 she was noted working in the Chinese coal trades but her aesthetic appearance had been seriously marred by the removal of nearly all masts and cargo gear. She was believed to be still active during March 2009.

The East German version of a Liberty Ship Replacement was built by VEB Schiffswerft 'Neptun' and aptly known as the *Neptun* type. A total of fifty-three *Neptun* ships were built between 1970 and 1985 but the series was subdivided into six similar types which gradually evolved from the initial *Neptun 381*, culminating with the slightly larger *Neptun 421*. The *421* design proved popular with ship owners, nearly all export customers, and represented almost two-thirds of the total *Neptun* series. Their versatility to carry a modest number of containers was an advantage. The *401* type was represented by the unique pair ***Hans Kruger*** and ***Annemarie Kruger*** (each 9019gt/76) built for Hans Kruger GmbH, West Germany. Following various name changes during the 1980s and early 1990s both ships were acquired by different Malaysian owners in 1995 and renamed ***Johan Crystal*** and ***Megah Jaya*** respectively. The pronounced long forecastle of the *Neptun 401* design, a distinguishing feature of the *388*, *403* and *421* types also, is noticeable in the picture of ***Megah Jaya*** at Singapore on 18 June 1997. She was sold to Chinese breakers in 2001. The ***Johan Crystal*** was subsequently renamed ***Samara***, ***Deneb*** and ***Spica*** before being scrapped at Chittagong in 2002.

One of the *Neptun 421* ships, built for former East German state-owned Deutfracht Seereederei VEB, carried the extraordinarily long name ***Fliegerkosmonaut Der DDR Sigmund Jahn*** (9231gt/79) as a tribute to East Germany's first cosmonaut. After German reunification in 1990, her name was pruned to ***Sigmund Jahn*** which she held until 1997 when renamed ***Loretta D*** following acquisition by Sounion Maritime Company Ltd, Liberia. On 27 May 2009 she anchored off Alang and soon afterwards was beached for scrapping. She is pictured, in container ship role, arriving at Cape Town 28 November 2005.

The *Neptun 403* was designed with distinctive central vertical posts for heavy-lift purposes. One of only three of this type the ***Cam Bubinga*** (9141gt/77) was launched as ***Ivory Uranus*** but completed for Cameroon Shipping Lines S.A., Cameroon. She traded between Douala, the Cameroon's principal port, and northern European ports until sold in 1987 to China Ocean Shipping Company (COSCO). She was renamed ***Yin Feng*** and allocated to regional subsidiary Dalian Container Steam Shipping Company. She is pictured in Manila Bay on 18 June 1998, minus her original 80-tonne heavy-lift derrick. Interestingly, the COSCO funnel colours she wears, albeit rather faded, were outdated by the late 1990s, having been supplanted in many of its vessels by a yellow base/blue top scheme (see ***Su Xia***, page 39).

The ***Yin Feng*** was renamed ***Bai An 6*** in 2003 and ***Jin Heng Hai*** prior to October 2005 when transferred to Dalian Jin Heng Shipping; by then she was the sole surviving *Neptun 403*. On 27 October 2005, she was photographed at one of Shanghai's coal berths, her appearance drastically altered by the removal of all masts and cargo gear for operating in the Chinese coal trades. At the end of March 2009 the ***Jin Heng Hai***, *Neptun 371* type ***Queen Haja*** (PAN, 8502gt/75), formerly ***Sol Neptun***, and twenty-one *Neptun 421*s were still in service. The ***Sinotrans Harmony*** (10018gt/84), formerly ***Mexica***, had arrived at Bijela, Montenegro, in July 2007 but was detained at the port because of litigation issues. There was no confirmation of the continued existence of three *Neptun 371* ships and *Neptun 421* type **Gumbong** (PRK, 10380gt/79), formerly ***Pacific Dragon***.

(Simon Smith)

The outstanding success of the *SD14*, *Freedom* and *German Liberty* designs to some extent eclipsed the introduction of other interesting Liberty Ship Replacement types from around the world, such as the British *Clyde* class. The *Clyde* was developed and marketed by Upper Clyde Shipbuilders Ltd (UCSL). Although aesthetically one of the least pleasing of the Replacement designs, it was nonetheless a sophisticated and versatile ship. Notably the standard specifications of the *Clyde* design included a beam of 75 feet (8 feet greater than the *SD14*) and a laudable container capacity of 450 TEU. After the first three *Clyde* vessels, ***Sig Ragne*** (GBR,11857gt/71), ***Samjohn Pioneer*** and ***Samjohn Governor*** (both 11506gt/1972), were delivered, construction work on four more for Haverton Shipping Ltd, London, was interrupted by the bankruptcy of UCSL. These ships were eventually completed in 1973. Two decades later ***Samjohn Pioneer*** was photographed on 17 June 1994 in the guise of Bahamas-registered ***Navick***, her fifth name. In the same year she was sold to another Bahamas concern and renamed ***Lady Charmain***. All seven *Clyde* ships had been sold to Indian or Chinese breakers by the end of 2001.

More than fifty Spanish Liberty Replacement *Santa Fe* type ships were completed in the 1970s, the majority by Astilleros Espanoles S.A. at Bilbao. Surprisingly, this yard completed twenty-five members for just one customer, Aegis Shipping Co Ltd, Greece. Many *Santa Fe* vessels had a length of 159 metres but some were built 12 metres shorter. There were also variations in the types of cargo gear fitted, ranging from all derricks to all cranes or a mixture of both. At least six ships were fitted with the latter arrangement including ***Aegis Blaze***. She is pictured as ***Al Faiha A*** (SYR, 11186gt/72) towards the end of her career off Tartous on 28 June 2001. She was the last surviving vessel of this group. Her final reported movement was in April 2002 when, under the Cambodian flag, she arrived at Calcutta probably for scrapping.

In March 2009 it was believed that no more than seven *Santa Fe* types remained active. One of the survivors, Chinese-owned ***Da Jiang Hai*** (9513gt/78), ex ***Qi Xia Shan***-03, ***Aegis Seaman***-79, is seen with her gear removed at the mouth of the Huangpu River in April 2004.

(Simon Smith)